# Praise for *The Innovation Revolution*

"If enterprise leaders want the spirit, secrets and success of startups translated to work inside big business, this is the one must-have book."

— **Andrew Hyde**, Founder of Startup Weekend

"For those of you with children, remember that obligatory gift we got, the "What to expect when you're first expecting?" Most made immediate intuitive sense (e.g. don't forget to change diapers often) while others were obscure bits of lore that you may not need now, but when you do, you're SUPER glad there's a reference.

Well, Kennedy's "Innovation Revolution" is the business equivalent for leaders navigating and driving in today's controlled chaos. Hyper-matrixed organizations with one official boss and 9 unofficial ones? Distributed budgeting and planning? Tension between digital natives and folks who knew a world without smartphones? All check. (Young people, that first scene in the original Ghostbusters featured what historians now call a "card catalog." Look it up in Wikipedia - that would be the ultimate in irony...).

This is the reality we all work in. Many of us are leaders today because we recognized how our teams can thrive in this context out of trial and error... and with a dash of luck. Boy, what I would have done for a rule book! Well, now we have one. Go read this and start your own movement."

— **Hideo Esaka**, Vice President, Client Systems Commercial Marketing, Dell Technologies

"Here is a powerhouse book on tips, tactics, and approaches to grow your business at warp speed using INTRApreneurs and the "smart speed method." Melissa Kennedy has written a thought provoking book on leadership and innovation for the 21st century."

— **Luanne Tierney,** Managing Member, Chief Marketing Officer, Fivesky

"Regardless of the size of your enterprise, change is here to stay and you have to embrace it if you're going to thrive. Knowing your employees, your key assets, and how to motivate them is going to be key in meeting business challenges. Embracing change and providing your employees a climate and culture to succeed will build a strong foundation for your longer-term objectives. Melissa provides some incredible insights to actions that we as leaders need to take to enable the innovation that will be required for the success of our employees and business."

— **Rick Bowers**, IBM Vice President & RTP Site Executive, IBM Cloud Technical Support

"The world is littered with dinosaur corporations who just can't find a way to innovate and as a result become less relevant every day. Could this be you? Today's best practices around startups can be yours as well. Simply take a read of this book and be both inspired to start as well as build a framework for effective innovation inside your company. I have been there through stints inside a $6B company, the federal government and as co-founder of MapQuest. The best business books are easy to consume and leave you with some great insights."

— **Chris Heivly**, Co-Founder of MapQuest (sold to AOL for $1.2B), Startup Evangelist, Investor

"This book reinforces essential leadership skills that every leader should be reminded of, regardless of how much experience they have. The situation-based applications for the many-faced Leadovator are especially powerful and practical. I've experienced working at every type of organization described in *The Innovation Revolution* (a Hierarchical Innovation Crusher, an Innovation Comeback Kid and a Nimble Innovation Powerhouse) – and the latter is, by far, the most exciting to be a part of!"

— **Lynn Vitello**, Vice President, Marketing, MaxPoint

"Finally! A text that embraces—rather than grimaces at—Millennials and their fast-paced, crowd-sourced, quick-decision, digital-denizen approaches as the next great stage in the evolution of effective business. From one person's idea, through the leanest of lean startups, to the rise and fall of behemoths we all know, Kennedy offers her hands-on, well-researched, tried-and-tested methods that not only span the range from entrepreneurial to intrapreneurial but from intimately introspective to explosively impactful."

— **Tim Flood,** Ph.D. Associate Professor, Management & Corporate Communication, UNC Kenan Flagler Business School, The Univeristy of North Carolina

"*The Innovation Revolution* is a resource treasure trove for managers who want to cut straight through the faddish jargon that plagues this topic and get down to doing business more creatively.

After reading it, they'll have at their disposal Melissa's level-headed breakdown of the latest research and best practices in innovation management and a clear--and quick--path to generating and strategizing ideas.

Melissa has no trouble with stalling, or stalled out creative plans. While her book attends to things like theories and cultural contexts, and generates richer and deeper action plans because of this, it's also obsessed with getting results.

To that end she equips her readers with tools, like individual and organizational diagnostics to help give them an informed and customized start; targeted practice exercises and challenges to help get things moving when moving is hard; an analysis of the physiology and cognition of mind-changing, because sometimes to work our brains we need to move our legs; a no-holds-barred management manifesto that will create time, flexibility, and the space for change within organizations; and diverse plans for overcoming all kinds of typical emotional, organizational, managerial, and personal obstacles.

Bottom line: you could attend all those innovation seminars, workshops, symposiums and MOOCs. Or you could read this book, and get started."

— **Dr. Colbey Emmerson Reid**, Consumer Innovation Collaborative, Director, Professor of Practice, NC State University, Poole College of Management

# THE INNOVATION REVOLUTION

Discover the Genius Hiding in Plain Sight

## K. Melissa Kennedy

# Dedication

For all who ever dared to change the world in the face of epic resistance; to those who have been bruised and brushed off; to those who show up with a brave heart and earnest intent; and to those who helped me make it all happen — my family, friends, power pals, champions, cheerleaders, fellow innovators, and rockstars — this book is for you.

# A Special Bonus from Melissa

With your copy of *The Innovation Revolution*, you are ready to inject the nimble, entrepreneurial spirit **back** into the enterprise with the genius hiding in plain sight.

Armed with proof of the complexity and intensity you face day-to-day, you know where to start, and where you must go. You are empowered to stand up and say NO to all that is impeding your path forward. AND, you are loaded with tools to make it happen.

For your courage to lead against business-as-usual, you deserve a little something special.

Here is my bonus gift for you:

- Discover your own hidden genius and ensure success with the digital workbook, **Activate Your Hidden Genius: 7 Surefire Actions to Ignite *The Innovation Revolution***
- Explore walking outside the lines and help make it stick with **The Weekly Zing**, an annual email subscription of weekly mini innovation exercises
- Take a simple **Three Little Orgs Innovation Assessment** to reveal your organization's innovation status and inform your next move

Go to http://innovationrevolutionbook.com/signup to access your bonus material.

Enjoy the ride in the driver's seat for your high speed, high impact journey to save the enterprise.

*It's on like Donkey Kong!*

Melissa

# Foreword

"If you can hear me, clap once!" A few of the 85 people clapped.
"If you can hear me, clap two times!!" Half of the crowd clapped twice.
"If you can hear me, clap three times!!!"
The entire crowd clapped three times and the meeting began.

It was January 2014 and I was at my first Triangle Interactive Marketing Association meeting. We were transitioning from the networking portion of the program and Melissa, who was the president, was our MC. In 15 seconds she had turned a room full of marketers with beer into a quiet and attentive audience. It was the first time that I met Melissa and we would serve on the board together for a year. Later we would help to organize Triangle Startup Weekend: Women, and now we co-host a Meetup for Design Thinking and Innovation.

Melissa is a force of nature! She is the personification of energy, enthusiasm and passion for getting things done. Whether working in the entrepreneurial community or hosting the VIP tent at Bonnaroo, she gives 100%.

When I read *The Innovation Revolution*, I heard her voice in every word. The book makes a cogent argument for the importance of returning innovation back to your organization. It is a carefully crafted system to return innovation where it belongs. I am old enough to have seen the first round of INTRApreneurship when Jack Welch was CEO of GE, and I have lived through Stagegate, Open Innovation, Lean Startup/Business Model Canvas, and Design Thinking. All of these are effective tools in your innovation toolkit, but nothing is as powerful as mobilizing all of your employees and their skills. Don't take my word on that. Melissa's work has led to more than $1 Billion in innovation pipeline for her clients. That's Billion with a B.

Every organization has people with great ideas that could change the company, but those ideas never seem to make it to the leadership team. Even when the ideas get to the C-suite they get stalled as just another innovation initiative. Melissa has laid out a plan to break through those impediments and innovate at the speed of the market so your company can build and maintain an advantage.

From the 360° Assessment to implementation and measurement, follow her plan to get your innovation efforts on track. Reflect on her observations about cultural and organizational obstacles that hamper an innovation culture. Most of all, reach out to her. She is a joyful woman who brings a Southerner's charm and compassion to every conversation. By the way, she may try to give you a tomato plant - it's a Southern thing.

Frank Pollock, President, The Pioneer Group

# Table of Contents

# Part 1

# 360° Reality Assessments

Any experienced leader or executive knows when launching a new initiative, the first step is assessing the current state of a situation.

*What happens today?*
*What are the driving forces?*
*Where are the opportunities?*
*Where are the obstacles?*

This investigative pursuit is in search of the most confident path forward.

You must start where you are. You must understand what and why in order to execute the how.

We will explore macro trends — speeding and shifting to an unruly new normal in business.

You will assess yourself, your organization, and your employees, and see where they fit into the transformation from siloed, spot innovation efforts to scalable systemic innovation. You will discover the path to becoming a **Leadovator** — a 21st century leader poised to deliver consistent innovative results at speed, by empowering others inside the enterprise to usher in *The Innovation Revolution*.

- Prepare for insights of why business-as-usual just won't work anymore.
- Review an 80s topic with a new context.
- Discover some quick steps to initiate your systemic ideas to action journey.

Your action adventure starts now.

- LEADOVATOR -
A 21st century leader
poised to deliver
consistent innovative
results at speed by
empowering others
inside the enterprise to
usher in The Innovation
Revolution.

# Chapter 1

## Dream No Longer, Embrace Your Leadership Responsibility, and Operationalize Innovation

*"A movement that changes both people and institutions is a revolution."*

— *Dr. Martin Luther King, Jr.*

Promise of the Chapter:

- Articulate the number one responsibility of the 21st century leader.
- Introduce the proven method to accelerate the transition to systemic innovation in the enterprise.

Imagine if you could ... injecting the best of the entrepreneurial world into your big corporate one to accelerate change and action through the talent you already have.

Imagine if you could ... skipping the corporate dance — you know the endless conference calls, dog and pony shows, and directionless spinning — and transform ideas into impact that drives consistent, exponential growth, at speed.

If you are thinking to yourself, *wouldn't that be nice* ... let me stop you. This is not a dream, an ideal or a nice-to-have. The ability to deliver consistent innovation with over-extended resources at speed is a leadership imperative for the future success of your enterprise.  I call these modern leaders Leadovators. Only these Leadovators, who operationalize change and innovation, will prevail. The rest won't matter.

Leaders in the Digital Information Age must have the ability to confidently make quick, calculated decisions based on massive amounts of imperfect information, combined with real customer-driven intel, at velocity. Leaders must adapt to the flattening of business that creates decision queues longer than *a Star Wars movie premier ticket line*. They must engage a growing, independent, and purpose-driven class of employees who are disrupting everything and leaving nowhere to hide in this digital age. AND, they must meet exponential growth expectations, despite complex competitive dynamics and dysfunctional, often linear, internal processes, and culture. This is a 21st century leader's *new normal*.

**Breathe**. There is a way to master this new leadership requirement and deliver, but it will take an open mind, a courageous heart and the ability to let go and empower from within.

Introducing the Smart Speed Method,™ a proven, rapid results method driven by employee INTRApreneurs that operationalizes innovation within the enterprise, and at a fraction of the time and costs of traditional strategy, planning, or innovation efforts.

*Speed to ideas.*
*Speed to decisions.*
*Speed to results.*
*Speed with empathy.*
*Speed with employee engagement.*
*Speed with intelligence and confidence.*

And it's within your reach.

That's the 21st century leadership responsibility — creating a systemic yet fluid business ecosystem, powered by trusted, talented people, ready to adapt and deliver at speed.

According to Ray Kurzwell's essay, *The Law of Acclerating Returns*, we will experience 20,000 years of progress in the 21 st century, instead of just the linear 100 years. (http://www.kurzweilai.net/the-law-of-accelerating-returns)

This accelerating evolutionary reality is upon us, and we are already behind. You feel it. You know it. The only way to meet such a monumental challenge is to start a movement, a revolution. Dr. Martin Luther King Jr. described it best when he said, *"A movement that changes both people and institutions is a revolution."* Welcome to *The Innovation Revolution*.

*Where to start?* Right where you are, right now. Who you are right now. The organization you work for today. The team you have. It all starts with the smallest step, and then another, and then another. Evolution doesn't happen overnight. It's the tiny tweaks that add up to big results. The hardest part is the start. Let's do this.

# Chapter 2

# The 21st Century Enterprise Leadership Reality

*"We can't solve our problems with the same thinking we used when we created them."*

*— Albert Einstein*

Promise of the Chapter:

- Understand my definition of innovation — "Change that Matters."
- Discover the key trends in today's business environment that reveal the 21st century leader's imperative to lead *The Innovation Revolution* for both survival and success.
- Reveal three quick-start actions to initiate your plan forward.

What do enterprise leaders experience today? *(This is the validation and head-nodding portion of the book.)*

- Information overload — more data and information than ever before in history.
- Growing, purpose-driven class of employees challenging everything: millennials and generation flux.
- Flattening business organization structures.
- Over-extended workforce where "Do more with less and less" is commonplace.
- A proliferation of project backlogs.
- Technology-enabled 'everything.'
- Plummeting "costs" of market entry — money and access.
- Exponential growth demands and intense pressure.
- Complex competitive and partner dynamics.

- Incongruent market expectations of startups vs. enterprise.
- Traditional management practices that hinder strategic agility and action.

Sound familiar? Is this your reality? If so, read on. If not, pass this book along to someone else; it won't help you.

With all that complexity and change, it's no wonder the leadership and management practices of the past aren't working. Need more proof they are waning in effectiveness?

Consider the fact that only 61 companies of the original Fortune 500 companies from 1955 survived. That's only 12.2%.[1]

Let's be clear. Big companies aren't the only ones at risk. The infamous, venture-backed billion dollar startups, known as unicorns, are dying faster than those 'Leave-it-to-Beaver' Fortune 500 companies. Venture Capitalist Jim Breyer predicts that only 10% of the 140 unicorn startup companies will survive. My favorite term for these soon-to-be extinct companies is "unicorpse," coined by Aileen Lee in *Welcome To The Unicorn Club, 2015: Learning From Billion-Dollar Companies*. Sadly, many of these companies are all hype and no profits. That's about the same amount as the Fortune 500 survival rate. Only difference? These businesses will fail faster.

All enterprises, regardless of size, require leaders who can quickly and confidently lead innovation — or as I define it, "change that matters" — within the complex unknown and at speed.

Don't get the wrong idea. This book isn't about fear mongering for corporate types. These are just 'proof points' consistently delivering innovation that drive real-live-no-jive results, and are the keys to success and survival.

Nothing stays the same, so the need to adapt and innovate is fundamental to success. Not just quarterly, annually, or within three to five years, but innovating as a constant. Innovation should be like breathing; it happens automatically without thinking about it. It's not about managing innovation and it's not about change management. It's about operationalizing innovation and change. That is the charge of the 21st century leader. Those that

---

[1] *https://www.aei.org/publication/fortune-500-firms-1955-v-2016-only-12-remain-thanks-to-the-creative-destruction-that-fuels-economic-prosperity/*

embrace their responsibility and lead *The Innovation Revolution* will be forever known as the Leadovator who saved the enterprise.

In order to discover a viable path forward, you must examine how you got here. What forces created this new paradigm of chaos? Only by understanding these dynamics can leaders build comfort in the uncomfortable and confidently deliver systemic innovation within the enterprise.

## Top 4 Trends Driving: *The Innovation Revolution*

Let's start with the changing demographics and dynamics of your workforce. The peeps who are turning the wheels while you steer.

Before we go any further, if you have the typical media-fed perception of "lazy, high maintenance" millennials, you need to let that go and open your mind to a different image. You need to activate your empathy and intellect, because, as Bob Dylan sings, "the times they are a changin'." Those 18-34 year olds now make up a third of today's workforce and are gaining experience and ground. If you continue your resistance to evolving with them, you will be left behind as others win the war on talent and progress. Millennials aren't the only disrupting force in your workforce. We will explore the effects of a psychographic group called Generation Flux,[2] described by Fast Company, and how these wonder twin groups are shaping the future[3].

## Trend 1: Millennial Madness, Generation Flux and the Big Quit

The workforce is in transition. Demographics and dynamics are changing rapidly. Baby boomers are retiring or at least want to and millennials are moving in. The generational divide comes with a different set of demands from employees. Millennials are demanding technology and automation over manual, labor-intensive solutions. In their DNA is the idea of less effort and more impact. Many come up with ideas and practices that cut standard operating procedures in half or more. This new crop of employees refuses to pretend they are working longer hours, and point to the outcomes versus hours invested. These attitudes and reactions, documented at length

---

[2] *https://www.fastcompany.com/section/generation-flux*
[3] *"Wonder twins" is a pop culture reference to The Wonder Twins, Zan and Jayna, are a fictional extraterrestrial twin brother and sister superhero duo who first appeared in Hanna-Barbera's American animated television series Super Friends. https://en.wikipedia. org/wiki/Wonder_Twins*

by Deloitte's 2016 Millennial Survey,[4] are creating a rift in the business-as-usual management practices, oh ... and driving leaders crazy in the process.

The millennial expectation of work environment and work impact differ from the thankful-I-have-a-job past. High tech, flexible, and fast are keywords millennials look for in job descriptions and interviews, according to leading recruiting news outlet ERE Media.[5] But those are just semantics. The millennial is not willing to blithely accept working with horrible bosses, a crushing workload, a lack of work-life balance, poor job satisfaction, or a general feeling like a cog in the wheel of a machine. The thundering demand of meaning and impact are rippling through the corporate world as millennials are willing to exit high-paying, big-title positions in search of respect and purpose.

Millennials aren't the only ones protesting this indentured servant-like working condition. Many brilliant, multi-generational employees who thrive in reinvention and disruption, sometimes called Generation Flux, also expect respect, autonomy, and appreciation. Both groups are putting their demands into action in what I call the "Big Quit" movement — a mind-blowing exit, despite an uncertain future. The U.S. Bureau of Labor Statistics keeps a detailed tally of employees who quit their jobs, and the numbers are telling. Despite a still-uncertain economy, people are quitting on their employers at a rate of more than 2 million each month.[6] Sure, plenty of those people are moving on to other positions. Yet a decent chunk of them are quitting because they are mad as hell and just can't take it anymore, to paraphrase the famous movie line from the popular 1970's movie *Network*.

The Big Quit harkens to the messages presented in the mid-19th century by Karl Marx and Friedrich Engels, who wrote *The Communist Manifesto*, which called on oppressed workers everywhere to unite and rise up against the chains of capitalism. In school, we all learned about this as one of the most powerful and enduring political doctrines in the world, one that gave rise to a form of government still followed by dozens of nations.

Maybe Marx and Engels were just two dudes who were fed up with their jobs. Maybe they experienced the crushing workload, fear-based motivational tactics, and the relentless metrics-based performance. Who knows, but what

---

[4] *https://www2.deloitte.com/global/en/pages/about-deloitte/articles/gx-millennials-shifting-business-purpose.html*

[5] *https://www.eremedia.com/tlnt/how-companies-can-best-recruit-and-retain-millennials/*

[6] *http://www.bls.gov/news.release/jolts.t04.htm*

we do know is that millennials are moving into the workplace in droves and other generations are echoing their sentiments. Today's employee expectations and actions are disrupting business-as-usual at an epic clip.

So what? These millennials and Gen Fluxers make up the talent pool all companies, large or small, compete for globally. Their expectations align with the pace and expectations your customers demand, too. One more thing: These millennials and Gen Fluxers are also your future customers. It's logical to assume they will also spend based on the same values they demand in their work. If you are not willing to adapt to recruit, empower and retain top millennial and Gen Flux talent, NOTHING will be delivered, much less world-changing innovations. Besides, going to work every day knowing your work has meaning and impact isn't a bad thing, right?

## Trend 2: "The D Word — Digitization"

This topic has been explained to death, so I will give you the skinny version. The digital revolution has accelerated the pace of change to hyper drive. Plus, those growing millennials and Gen-Fluxers speak digital fluently and can help leaders and their organizations alike navigate and capitalize on this trend. They are your secret weapon in your quest to operationalize innovation.

Digitization has driven access. Access to information, to resources, talent, to code, to customers, to the globe, and beyond. And as things (Internet of Things, #IOT) [7] and people become more connected the pace will only speed up.

Digitization has driven data. "Big data," as it's called, offers algorithms for predictive analytics and modeling to better inform future actions. We are in an unprecedented era of tracking. You can't even walk into your kitchen without your technology counting your steps.

Digitization has driven automation, or what some assume is the magical cure-all. Computer-driven cranes and machines can now build things like the pyramids that required legions of people. Technology is self-generating intelligence, now becoming smarter than the creator. Automation is essential to meeting the needs of the marketplace, as the sheer volume of workers shrink in size.

Digitization has driven chaos in the enterprise. It has created the concept of frenemies, competitors who are also partners. The USPS, UPS, and FedEx [8]

---

[7] https://en.wikipedia.org/wiki/Internet_of_things
[8] US Registered trademarks

are a classic example of frenemies. The USPS can deliver to the most rural of locations, while UPS and FedEx have the capacity to ship odd-shaped and giant packages. They all must work together to deliver despite their competitive status.

Digitization eliminates the permanent. Since you can update on-the-fly, upgrade overnight, and tweak if there is a bug or mistake, there is no real state of permanence in the new digital world. As soon as something is released, it is out-of-date. That applies to your competitive advantage too. Once it's out in the world, someone is going to build on it or steal it. Embracing and capitalizing on change at speed is the only way to stay ahead in this new disposable environment.

Digitization has created scale. Consider how Amazon went from online book retailer to Walmart's biggest retail competitor, without opening a single brick and mortar store. Digitization has highlighted change and uncertainty in a big, fat, BOLD, hot pink highlighter. Change is the only true constant in this equation. We pretend that with all our track-ability, data modeling, automation, and access that we have a solid foothold on the future. That, my friend, is a fallacy.

**- FRENEMIES -**
Friends and Competitors

My simple proof of this fallacy can be summed in one word: Snapchat.® The massively popular video and messaging app is a metaphor for the modern world. It enables users to move quickly to the next thing, making the last thing irrelevant. It feeds the beast and scratches the relentless itch for newer, faster, more. That's exactly how we're living now, and it's so counter to the thought patterns of previous generations. Before, you wouldn't put effort into something that would disappear in a matter of seconds or 24 hours.

Digital technology has made the world a digital, disposable, temporary place. However, the fact remains people are still a part of the enterprise. We haven't gotten to the "Skynet" era that the 1984 movie *Terminator* created. Although Google® is coming close.

*Warning spoiler alert:* no one wants that machine-dominated world—at least not the James Cameron version.

Digitization has accelerated change, created a false sense of stability, and offered unparalleled access to more markets, models, and money. In order to lead successfully in the 21st century, leaders must master digital fluency on the path to operationalizing innovation. Digitization affects everything in the enterprise, including organization structures, internal processes, employee, customer engagement, and beyond. No vision of the future is accurate without a digital lens. Leaders who superficially acknowledge this essential trend without gaining a deep understanding of its application, will fade into irrelevancy for the growing millennial and Gen Flux talent, the empowered consumer class, and, frankly, everyone else too.

## Trend 3: Risk Mitigation Addiction & the Wisdom of the Unpredictable

Blame it on shareholders and trigger-happy stock markets. Blame it on the big data modeling movement. Blame it on our own insecurities as a species. Regardless, everyone yearns for certainty. We have become addicted to risk mitigation — defined as taking steps to reduce adverse effects. Everyone strives to reduce risk at all cost. And sometimes that cost is the unpredictable innovation that transforms a business or the world. But our overwhelming addiction blinds us to the possibility and thus impedes progress, suspends decisions, and sometimes destroys our very existence.

Here is the thing. Human beings are essential to business today. Humans are irrational. Just ask anyone who has taken an ECON 101 class. The number one reason we can't predict economic certainty for the stock market is the fact that humans are irrational. They don't always do what the data predicts. There is, however, sometimes wisdom in the unpredictable. That is how innovation is discovered, nurtured, and released into the wild. If people are involved, change, uncertainty, and often genius is every organization's bedfellow.

People are messy. Working with other people is awesome or awful. It's not easily boiled down to a clever Mad Men-like tagline or elegant responsive web design. It's gnarly. People avoid gnarly because it's hard. People will take the path of least resistance every time. It's one of the laws of nature. And, because it is messy, unpredictable and hard, we all avoid it.

Organizations have lost their humanity knowingly or unknowingly because of the obsessive need for certainty. We are constantly trying to remove human error and, sometimes, human input in service of reaching a state of risk-free nirvana. But here is a little secret: humans are the ones buying your products and services. Humans are the decisions makers. Humans create the PO or pay by credit card. Therefore, the very thing you are pining to destroy is the one thing that allows you to exist.

Our addiction to certainty, risk mitigation and denial of the unpredictability of humanity in the workplace drives bad business behaviors that are crushing your potential.

**Top Three Bad Business Behaviors, driven by our risk-mitigation obsession:**

1. The big one — **legacy inertia.**[9] This is the old status quo — business-as-usual. This is the concept that organizations stick with — the same process, tech, people, and solution because they know the outcome. It isn't necessarily the best outcome, yet the need to know exactly what will happen outweighs the risk of trying something new. These dysfunctional internal processes are weighing you down, slowing you down, and driving talent into the arms of nimble, innovative leaders who get it. This internal dysfunction is so evident to corporate leaders, they are all rushing to create these startup teams outside the normal business operation to isolate the risk, innovate at speed, and remove the crushing weight of the over-processed state of the enterprise.

2. Enterprises spend millions with BIG, old-guard strategy consulting firms. No one got fired for hiring a McKinsey, Bain, or Accenture. It gives us options like the handy **blame cord** if their recommendations don't work, but at the cost of speed and internal genius. Before the Internet, that investment was legitimate because information of cross function or industry best practice wasn't one Google search away, but not anymore. The continued reliance on old-guard strategy consultants is not the move of a Leadovator. Application of knowledge is worth that million dollar price tag, not the knowledge itself. Hiring "the old-guard experts" suggests it is more important to have an escape hatch for the wrong move to save your personal bacon, than it is to bravely lead innovation by embracing failure as learning and inspiring others to do the same. You can't expect anyone to take risks if leaders aren't willing to take them.

3. It drives us into the arms of the *Appegeddon*, the era where there *seems* to be an app for everything. We pay for unneeded software because we think it will solve our problems. We oversimplify and perpetuate a check-box mentality, instead of doing the root cause analysis and transformational work necessary for real sustainable change. Ironically, you still need people to interact with that software. That seemingly small investment actually has a big hidden cost. The cost of adoption — you know, the masses of people communicating, incentivizing, pestering, and threatening others to use the software.

---

[9] *The term legacy inertia was developed by my pal and CEO David Rose. It's genius. Thanks for letting me use it David!*

These three common bad business behaviors are at the core of your dysfunction, and it is all in service of our need to mitigate risk. Don't feel bad about this addiction to risk mitigation or certainty, everyone has it. No one wakes up and says, "Gee, I can't wait to see what changes are in store today." No one! To demonstrate the pervasive nature of change, think about the fact that when you woke up this morning, some feature on one of your apps has changed or gigabits of new information, videos, and data were uploaded or downloaded-all in the time it takes you to hit the snooze button. It's overwhelming. The information crush and the speed of change are intimidating for EVERYONE. But you are a leader, and it is your responsibility to courageously set the example so others may follow.

Do you now see how business-as-usual just won't do? To quote the legendary innovator Albert Einstein, "We can't solve our problems with the same thinking we used when we created them." Change is constant. Control is imaginary. Humans are essential to progress. And the promise of full-proof risk mitigation is not only false, it is also a full frontal of fear within leaders sending the "do as I say, not as I do" signal to your entire organization. By the way, the fact that millennials and Gen-Fluxers challenge this type of hypocrisy may be the very reason they frustrate you so much.

An effective, well-respected 21st century leader must accept the risk, uncertainty, and fluidity of today's business landscape and empower talent inside and across the matrix of stakeholders to deliver results-bearing innovations, without 100% assurances. It is not a task for the faint of heart, or the fearful. It is, however, an absolute for successful leadership of the future.

## Trend 4: The Startup Revolution and the Age of Entrepreneurship

There is no denying startups have fundamentally changed the way business works, creating advantages from bold, yet "unfair" practices, new income streams, funding and valuation models, and new workplace norms, like co-working environments, no vacation policies, candy walls, and Tequila Tuesdays. Enterprise leaders are conflicted. On the one hand, they are green with envy of the speed, agility, guts, and the "cool" factor. On the other, they are concerned with the impact on their marketplace positions and the radical change necessary to compete effectively.

It all started back in the mid 1990s when serial entrepreneur, investor, and advisor Steve Blank introduced a genius new Customer Development framework that focused more on the business and marketing side of start-ups vs. the traditional, all-in focus on the engineering and product development side. He argued the need to balance customer needs with product development. It sounds like the same old stuff, but with a twist — a scientific approach of iterative development and testing in almost real time. Instead of long development cycles and little customer input, he introduced the beginnings of the lean startup methodology.

Then in the early 2000s, he and Eric Ries further developed this Customer Development framework into the now almost ubiquitous Lean Startup movement, combined with the methodologies that match up Blank's customer development framework with concepts of lean manufacturing and create a fast, cheap, iterative cycle of development, release, measure, and develop again. It's now a global movement guiding millions of entrepreneurs and thousands of startups.

THE LEAN STARTUP PROCESS BY ERIC RIES

LEARN

IDEAS

BUILD

MINIMIZE THE
TOTAL TIME THROUGH
THE LOOP

DATA

CODE

MEASURE

The Lean Startup movement, combined with the open source movement and inexpensive startup production costs, provides the now famed startup revolution that introduced an epic disturbance in the corporate world.

Splashed across pages of Wired, Fast Company and Gizmodo, are tiny start-ups eating big corporate giants for lunch with faster, more relevant releases at lower costs, because of infinitely smaller infrastructures and a fluid adaptive mindset.

Community advocate programs for these entrepreneurs gave support in a way that legitimized the pursuit of a different path. The startup stories changed from two founders in a garage to many finding each other through entrepreneurial community events, co-working spaces, free education seminars, boot camps, and mentor programs. The community support didn't just help these entrepreneurs start; they created natural paths to help scale through incubators, accelerators, and continued advance mentoring programs.

On top of all of those programs and support, these communities promoted entrepreneurship as a means for economic development and job creation, at a time when the US was experiencing its worst recession since the Great Depression. Jobs, especially for white collar, educated people, and those fresh out of college, a.k.a. the rising millennial talent class, were scarce. The political and media coverage helped elevate the path of entrepreneurship as a means to save the economy and the world. It removed any prevailing stigma, which was the boost these brave founders needed to take the plunge. Plus, with no jobs available, what did these people have to lose? This movement serves as a beacon of hope and validation to this dismissed, rising millennial workforce, that flexibility, impact, and meaning in work is possible and profitable.

Finally, the capital, the money to help startups scale, became readily available. Investors of all types bought into the media frenzy and wanted in. They had seen this before when the dot.com companies lined many investors' pockets. Add to that the relatively cheap cost of capital with super low interest rates, and it created the perfect storm to usher in the startup revolution.

The democratization of innovation began. Anyone could start a company. It led to recognized, billion dollar, publicly-traded giants like Facebook and Box, to billion dollar-valued private companies like AirBnB® and Uber®. No one really knows how many startups have emerged from this movement. According to the Global Entrepreneurship Monitor, some 305 million companies have started in the last 15 years globally[10].

---

[10] *http://www.gemconsortium.org/*

While there is a proliferation of startups, 80-90% fail. And, the ones that have made it are shaking traditional business models. Nimble, agile, and gaining ground, these companies play by a different set of rules. They can pivot or change course on a dime, while the giants are in slow motion. They have incongruent market expectations from well-established companies — their valuations are based on user growth, not necessarily revenue growth, and most of the time they don't have to be profitable.

How on earth can established companies compete when they are held to a higher standard of sustainability and solvency? They must first admit they have legacy systems, dysfunctional organization structures and processes, and shareholder demands, which hinder speed and action. They must stop choosing the sexy, yet temporary fixes of acquisition and old-guard consulting recommendations. They must face their bias against fixing the gnarly complex inside and step up and lead the change necessary to survive and thrive.

Today's leaders must challenge the problematic norms that served as platforms for success of the past. They must do the burdensome work of transitioning and transforming from within, vs. starting with a blank slate. Starting from nothing is easier than transitioning from something. Legacy and history are far more powerful than the shiny possibility of brand new. It's like restoring a classic car; you don't want to change the very thing that made it classic in the first place. On the other hand, if you can't drive it, is it really worth much?

Layer these four disruptive trends on top of the usual maddening issues facing leaders, such as resource shortages, project backlogs, reaction-only mode, and siloed, opposing functional goals, and you understand the 21st century leader's reality. And the responsibility to usher continuous innovation at speed among all the complexity, or disappear within the cyclone of change.

Whoa, that's enough to make you increase your lottery play. Instead of taking that gamble, let's explore:

*How to adapt to face the new normal.*
*How to begin the enterprise evolution.*
*How to lead the charge in The Innovation Revolution.*

You must start by recognizing your business-as-usual habits first; then you will discover the opportunity and the path forward within all this disruption.

### First Three Actions to get started:

1. **Embrace** these changes as the new reality, not some flash-in-the-pan blip, and begin to recognize them at play.
2. **Recognize** my definition of innovation: Change that Matters.
3. **Prepare** yourself for a personal evolution riddled with fear and uncertainty, but rewarded with a revolution that will change the world.

And so it begins, a change in outside forces requires a change inside. Control is a myth, and change as a constant is the reality.

# THE Weekly ZING

## Your Innovation Challenge
## R&D

Practice a little "R&D"
No…not research and development, but rip and duplicate.

Best practices or personal experience are powerful and innovative sources of information and knowledge to apply.
Look at your favorite consumer brand -- be that Coke, Tesla or Angry Birds and try out something they have done in your work environment. After all, imitation is the highest form of admiration.

Share your best R&D idea with @48Innovate use #R&D.

# Chapter 3

# Your Control Among the Chaos: You & Your Actions

*"We are what we repeatedly do."*

*— Aristotle*

Promise of the Chapter:

- Understand 21st century leader attributes to successfully lead *The Innovation Revolution.*
- Assess your dominant leader archetype.
- Discover the CURE to evolving and thriving in the new normal.

Leaders come in all shapes, sizes, and styles. There is no shortage of personality tests, strengths finder exercises or BuzzFeed-like listicles of top qualities found within successful leaders. It's starting to feel like the dissection of successful leadership is more like a scientific alien probe than a productive pursuit of discovery, but knowing is half the battle.

In order to master the ability to lead, develop and deliver innovation at speed systematically, you must challenge your assumptions and expectations that influence your actions. That is no small feat.

It takes observation, recognition, contemplation and decisive action and then, constant reevaluation and adaptation. You and your actions and reactions are the only thing you have control over.

Remember, you don't just have one Eureka moment; instead you have a million Eureka moments among a constant flow of doubt, confusion and discomfort.

> In order to master the ability to lead, develop and deliver innovation at speed systematically, you must challenge your assumptions and expectations that influence your actions.

Innovation by nature is fluid and, therefore, you should learn to be fluid too. And since you hold a leadership position, it is your responsibility to lead your team and organization by example.

Let's explore you and your leadership type. Everyone has proclivities. They are neither wrong nor right, just tendencies that can be complemented to accelerated results.

First a little fun. You and your friends meet up to go to a concert. Someone brings an extra person with a ticket not in your section. What would you do?

   a.  Take the single ticket yourself and give your ticket to the extra person, suggesting that since you are shorter and find it difficult to see over the crowd, the new seat location is better for you.
   b.  Negotiate with someone sitting around the group to trade tickets.
   c.  Say, "sorry dude, we don't have any extra tickets in our section, but we will meet you after."

Remember your answer to this one. It may be more revealing of your inner leadership persona than you think.

**Three Attitude and Motivation Archetypes of Leaders:**

1. **Pleaser**
2. **Explorer**
3. **Imperialist**

## Extreme Executives Walk Into a Bar

**The Pleaser Type:** Bobby Ewing, SouthFork Rancher Owner and former CEO of Ewing Oil and a lead character in the hit US television TV series *Dallas*.

**The Explorer Type:** Peggy Olson, secretary turned copywriter turned copy editor in the hit cable TV show, *Mad Men*.

**The Imperialist Type:** Francis Underwood, House Whip turned default US President in the hit Netflix series *House of Cards*.

Bobby Ewing
"Pleaser"

Peggy Olson
"Explorer"

Francis Underwood
"Imperialist"

## Scenario:

Bobby Ewing, Frank Underwood, and Peggy Olsen walk into a bar. The inexperienced bartender says, *"We haven't restocked the bar from that wicked Tesla launch party last night, so we are only serving coffee or Gin Fizzes. What can I get for you?"*

Bobby Ewing says, *"I don't really like Gin Fizzes, but if that's what you are serving, I guess I will have a Gin Fizz."*

Frank Underwood says, *"I can't believe you call this a bar, this is unacceptable. I will take Gin on the rocks and make it a double for the same price since you gave me no other option. Deal?"*

Peggy Olson pauses and looks around the bar. She walks over to a few other patrons, and there is a boisterous discussion. She comes back and says, *"Well if you have seltzer in that soda machine, use those limes in that centerpiece over there, and use those sugar packets for the coffee, and make me a Gimlet please."*

Bobby, Frank and the bartender look puzzled.

Peggy says, *"I asked the others in the bar to look around and come up with all the cocktail combinations with the ingredients that are in sight. They came up with tons of options. I picked the Gimlet from the list. You want me to bring them over to share some options with you?"*

Everyone ended up with a beverage, but Peggy used all her resources at her disposal to get what she *wanted*. It's a lesson even experienced leaders can learn from, especially as they try to navigate today's disruptive business environment.

You, as a leader, have such power. You have the ability to transform. You are the most important factor to productivity and results for your organization. In 2015, Gallup released a study[11] finding that about 50% of the 7,200 adults surveyed left a job "to get away from their manager." That's right, more than 50% of employees leave because of their manager. While staggering, frightening, and disappointing, it is also powerful. And, as Uncle Ben from Spiderman said, "With great power comes great responsibility," ... to your employees, your company, and your customers. You, as the manager, a.k.a. leader, are the fulcrum between your employees and organizational success. Hence why you must develop and empower your team and organization to adapt and deliver at speed. *No pressure.*

---

[11] *http://fortune.com/2015/04/02/quit-reasons/*

The study cited that employees listed lack of clear direction and expectations being the number one frustration point. This demand for clarity will only increase, as challenges and opportunities become more ambiguous. The black and white world of yesterday is gone forever, so if you didn't master communicating clear expectations then — watch out — it's about to get harder. It will be essential for you to present clarity within ambiguity, and here is what you face:

- Today's business environment is complex global, local, matrix.
- Everything is constantly changing in near real-time.
- Information and misinformation are flying around like meteors along Orion's Belt with no time or discipline to discern the truth or the relevant.
- Siloed organizations with intense pressure to deliver use data to support their goals ONLY, not necessarily in service of the seamless customer experience essential to win.
- Incentive and reward structures don't align with the matrix reality nor do they offer intrinsic motivators.
- Everyone is over-extended, wired and tired, which makes the simplest of tasks and insights impossible.
- Complicate all the above with a side of humanity — the imperfect, the diverse, and the different among all talent up and down the corporate hierarchy.

It's clear as mud. This chaos is not your fault. The work environment changed faster than our ability to manage it. Traditional command and control methods of the past don't adequately create the agile, trusting environment that allows for the nimble, clear reset necessary to rally your teams to seize opportunities quickly. Plus, you (the collective you and your organization) are rewarded for hitting the targets you promise, not for unexpected outcomes, positive or negative.

If our reliable, traditional methods are choking innovation and leaking talent needed to deliver, what is a leader to do? A real-live-no-jive innovative leader's dilemma.

As a leader in today's light-speed, digital, chaotic, uncertain, hyper-competitive, and collaborative business environment, it is imperative for you to master managing and delivering innovation at warp speed. You must be able to set and reset direction clearly and at speed so your teams can bring their best talents to help the organization win. Your survival depends on it. I am not pulling a *Chicken Little* here; I am stating a fact.

There are several characteristics, behaviors and skills of a Leadovator-- a 21st century leader poised to deliver innovative results consistently at speed by empowering others. You don't have to have a big fancy title to be a Leadovator, but you do have to have the right attitude, apply the right skills and take bold actions to succeed. It's time you take a moment and look within and assess your attitudes, aptitude and actions. Self-awareness is the only way to define your path forward.

## Three ingredients make up the leader profile:

- Attitudes
- Aptitude
- Actions

## Assess your Attitude

You must first inspect your attitudes and motivations to deliver. This will serve as your ground zero or starting point on your transformational journey to Leadovator.

| Leader Attitude Archetypes | Common Attitudes and Actions |
|---|---|
| Pleaser | Embraces empathy, seeks approval of others, finds it difficult to express true feelings and thoughts, fears rejection |
| Explorer | Embraces uncertainty, acts selflessly to do the right thing, engages in dialogue not debates |
| Imperialist | Delivers no matter what, Uses I/Me/My frequently, dislikes bad news, strives to be in charge |

Your assignment is to notice. Notice in every interaction if any of these attitudes are present. When you communicate with your employees, are you trying to seek their or your executive's approval? Do you use I/Me/My frequently? When making decisions do you give up a short-term gain for exponential gain later?

All leaders tend to exemplify attitudes of all archetypes; your assignment is to determine which is your dominant persona. What is your instinctual reaction?

## Assess Your Aptitude

Regardless if it is natural aptitude or learned skills, leaders who successfully make the leap to Leadovator and usher persistent employee innovation at speed within organizations must leverage and learn. Take inventory of your capability portfolio and recognize if you need to augment with Leadovator ones.

| Top Pleaser Aptitudes | Top Explorer Aptitudes | Top Imperialist Aptitudes | Top Leadovator Aptitudes |
|---|---|---|---|
| Management by objective | Recognizes his/her limitations | Delegation | Digital fluent |
| Project management | Ability to let go, adapt | Recruiting | Analysis |
| Consensus-building | Prioritizes experimentation and learning | Developing Key Performance Indicator (KPI)/ metrics | Problem solving |
| Ethics | Embraces uncertainty and ambiguity | Providing direction | Resource management across the matrix of stakeholders |
| Reporting | Collaborative | Find and leverage quick wins | Clear communication despite imperfect information and ambiguity |

## Assess Your Actions

### Ten Top Leadovator Actions for the 21st Century:

1. Engages in dialogue not debates.
2. Inspires curiosity and rebellion against the status quo.
3. Demonstrates resiliency and converts failure into learning, sharing mistakes openly, creating a safe, trusting environment.
4. Drives discipline, accountability, and execution.
5. Eliminates obstacles, non-productive bureaucracy, and emphasizes adaptation at speed through experimentation.
6. Communicates, clearly and transparently, stretch goals, strategic direction, and feedback.
7. Embraces uncertainty.
8. Builds boundaries not borders through co-management principles and cross-functional inclusion.
9. Infuses the team with passion, confidence, and motivational energy.
10. Balances analytics with a decision-making framework for themselves and the team.

- *How do your actions stack up against this list?*
- *Do you consistently take these actions in your daily work life?*

## *What's Your Dominant Leader Identity?*

Below is a fun assessment to help you determine your dominant leader identity. Remember, there is no right answer to these questions. Be honest with your selections. The only way for you to define your path forward is to understand where you are starting.

1. Your company mandates all LinkedIn™ profiles must have a green background for a consistent employer brand presence. *What would you do?*
   a. Just do it.
   b. Get a group together to come up with a creative way to use a green background as a "green screen" treatment so employees can display your favorite thinking spot at the office.

    c. Spin people up in debate of why we shouldn't do it.

2. You are put in charge of the weekly managers meeting because your manager is on vacation. *What would you do?*

    a. Hold the meeting as regularly scheduled.

    b. Poll the team to seek input on the agenda, whether to move the meeting to Wednesday or shorten the meeting.

    c. Add some self-serving agenda items and move the meeting to the conference room closest to your office.

3. You are a week from a big launch and you learn that the materials needed for the launch are delayed because of a fire with your supplier in China, and delivery will be delayed by at least a month. *What would you do?*

    a. You blame the delay on the fire, emphasizing it was out of your control.

    b. You take responsibility for the delay. You leverage the opportunity to revise future launch plan requirements to increase lead times for material orders and diversify the supplier community.

    c. Find a domestic supplier who will supply the materials at triple the cost. Take credit for solving the short-term solution and send a memo describing how you saved the day.

4. You have a weekly project check-in meeting. *How many times do you allow an employee to miss a deliverable within one business quarter?*

    a. Ten to twelve misses in a quarter. You say, *"that's ok, I know you're busy and have lots on your plate."*

    b. It depends on what task was missed and the impact it makes on the project. The number isn't really the issue.

    c. 1-3 misses in a quarter. Everyone has a "miss" and we need this completed in order to meet the demands of our customers.

5. You want to start using Basecamp™ as a project-management standard. In order to make this move effective, you need 3 departments to agree on the move. *What would you do?*

    a. You whip up your finest Powerpoint™ presentation detailing the benefits and hit the normal socialization tour, going door to door to get to yes from the 3 departments.

b. You hold an hour meeting that suits most decisions makers' schedules to facilitate buy-in and follow up with individuals that were on vacation during the meeting to explain and confirm acceptance.

c. You hold only one meeting led by Basecamp sales representatives and commit to the deal at the end.

6. One of your previous flagship products is being retired. *How do you communicate this tough message?*

   a. Explain what you need to do, how to do it and why it's important. Invite the team to share their frustration and then ask them to rally behind the decision.

   b. Explain the situation and why we are doing this. Ask the team how we should accomplish this transition and still maintain loyalty of our customers.

   c. Just do it. Here is exactly what we need to do and when the transition will be complete.

7. You've just learned there is a new regulation that may impact your next product roll out. *What would you do?*

   a. Worry and lose sleep about all the possibilities.

   b. Bring the team together, and generate "What if" scenarios and options over pizza.

   c. Hold off on launch until the outcome is clear. You don't want to attach your name to a potential failure.

8. You are opening a new office in Hong Kong and you've been told to pick your top players to be a part of the startup team. *What would you do?*

   a. Ask who on the team wants to be on the startup team.

   b. Negotiate new measurable objectives with the management team after explaining the trade off of sending your best team members to lead the effort. Send your top two members to lead the charge.

   c. Select two team members that will have the least impact to your team's performance.

9. How do you start a meeting?

   a. I check in with each person and how they are feeling about their work.

   b. I start with a team cheer.

   c. I have a clear agenda, expectations and timelines.

10. You need to grow the business by 10%. You have customer data, histori-
    cal data and top industry trends. The team is split between two options.

*How do you decide?*

   a. Continue the discussion until the team reaches consensus.
   b. Have two teams pitch to a cross-functional panel of judges to decide
      the go forward plan.
   c. Decide for the team by selecting the quickest option to results.

Now it's time to score to reveal your dominant innovation leader identity.

## Scoring Key:

a = 1 point,  b = 3 points,  c = 5 points

Add them up and see your score.

If you scored between 10 and 21 points, you most identify with the
"Pleaser" leader archetype. You prioritize team consensus. Your empathy
and understanding are your powerhouse strengths. You rely on the story
behind decisions, actions and team dynamics to help you lead. Your top
aptitudes include collaboration, project management, and reporting. You
are well liked and can leverage those relationships in a pinch. Sometimes
you get caught up in the story of your employees or circumstances of a
situation. You have tendency to get stuck in the details and numbers that
causes some decision hesitation.

If you scored between 22 and 40 points, you most identify with the
"Explorer" leader archetype. You prioritize inclusivity, creativity and prag-
matism. Your ability to bring diverse opinions to help make decisions and
level-set changes in circumstances allows you to push some boundaries.
Your top aptitudes include empowering employees, setting limitations to
help the collective succeed and demonstrating that failure is only another
form of education. Sometimes you get caught up in the fairness of a situation and can lose the political game for a more long-term vision. You have
a tendency of big thinking that might miss the short-term mark needed to
get to the next level.

If you scored between 41 and 50, you most identify with the "Imperialist"
leader archetype. You prioritize facts and rapid results. You have proven
your ability to get stuff done despite most circumstances. Your top aptitudes

include delegation, recruiting resources and leveraging quick wins to get ahead. Sometimes you get caught up in your own reputation and success and may inadvertently dismiss others in the process. Your quick fire nature can leave some opportunities on the table.

Remember the answer you choose in the beginning of the chapter around the concert ticket dilemma? Does it match with your dominant leader archetype? A = Pleaser, B = Explorer, C = Imperialist. Your reactions are ingrained in your whole self, not just your role as a leader or manager. They are a culmination of your experiences and now form habitual patterns in all aspects of your life. Let me be infinitely clear, there are no right or wrong reactions, only the right decision or action at the right time, place or circumstance.

It is important to note that each of these leader archetypes come in handy in different situations. Recognizing your habitual leader reactions will be key in playing the right part at the right time in order to lead *The Innovation Revolution* and leapfrog the competition.

Now that you know which leader archetype you lean toward, here is your Leadovator CURE and your assignment for the next 30 days.

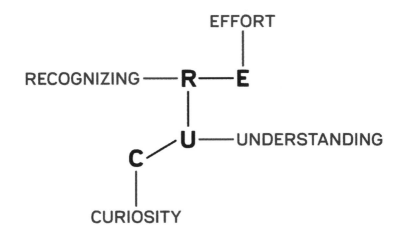

C = Curiosity

U = Understanding

R = Recognizing

E = Effort

**C**uriosity. You must have the desire to boost your innovation leader dexterity and be willing to question all your habitual management views and patterns. Inquisitively observe mentors, peers or employees to see if they possess any of the attitudes, aptitudes, or actions these Leadovators have. Don't be afraid to question the norm.

**U**nderstanding. Your curious questioning of business-as-usual may lead you into unfamiliar territory. Perhaps you never thought of or through a certain process of your experience on one project. You vowed never to question an executive, for example, because you were later reprimanded. You need to investigate and understand *why* you have formed all these habits on your journey to Leadovator. You will find some traumatic or successful results have led you to developing habits that are no longer valid. Understand why you do something; then assess if it still serves you as a leader in this transformational era.

**R**ecognizing. Your next challenge is to recognize when you are relying on normal habits. Once you are curious enough to see what you or others do, and then understand why you do them, it's now time to recognize and realize when you are on "autopilot."

**E**ffort. Now it's time for action. Your curiosity has lead to an understanding of why you do certain things. You are recognizing when those situations come up and noticing them. Now it's time to do something about it. Take three leadership habits and create a plan. When they come up, notice, pause, and implement your change action. Practice these three changes over and over until the new habit forms.

You can apply this **CURE** formula to all of your attitudes, aptitudes, and actions in order to recognize old habits, form new ones, and evolve and adapt at hyper-speed.

In the next chapter, you will assess if your organization can transition from a hierarchical, change-averse empire, to a collaborative, nimble powerhouse of innovation.

"It's a long and winding road," as the Beatles sang. Before you set out on that trek, it's best to know if it will lead to the innovation destination you seek.

<sup></sup>THE **Weekly ZING**

## Your Innovation Challenge
## Curious George

Most innovative people are
highly observant and curious.

Take an existing process and ask
5 questions on why you do it that way and
observe what comes up.

Share your insights with @48Innovate use
#curiousgeorge.

# Chapter 4

# Reality Check. Hierarchical Innovation Crusher vs. Nimble Innovation Powerhouse

*"Our choices define us."*

*— Rose Marcario, CEO, Patagonia*

Promise of the Chapter:

- Define three types of organizations relative to innovation.
- Provide assessment tools to evaluate your organization.
- Offer practical actions to take to ensure your environment supports your Leadovator mission.

Organizational environment and culture is a Leadovator's platform for operationalizing innovation at speed and leading *The Innovation Revolution*. Before investing your time and energy into this transformation, you must evaluate the viability of these efforts within your own organization.

*Does your organization have the capacity to evolve to this new normal and seize the future?*

## Three Types of Organizations, when it comes to innovation:

1. **Nimble Innovation Powerhouse:** Organizations that have it and want to continue to grow it.
2. **Innovation Comeback Kid:** Organizations that were innovative and lost it, but can still make a comeback.
3. **Hierarchical Innovation Crusher:** Organizations that got lucky, but can't innovate or survive in the future.

## Three Little Orgs

**Nimble INNOVATION POWERHOUSE**

**INNOVATION comeback -KID-**

**Hierarchical INNOVATION -CRUSHER-**

Anytime you categorize something, there is always a scale. There are no absolutes. Organizations and companies are no different.

**Scenario 1: This little org went to market.** Take AirBnB® for instance, an organization that definitely has innovation running through its veins. This genius organization is basically the largest hotel chain in the world and owns no property. Not resting on these laurels, AirBnB® is going after commercial office space next, and yet still owns no property. This organization has it and wants to continue to grow it. Don't over rotate. Remember this innovation darling isn't all glory. It faces some major hurdles by ignoring regulations and overlooking potential discriminating rental policies. Innovation at speed, without being smart, has consequences, too. However, leaders in this company have the ability to look beyond and rally their people to execute, despite the headwinds of change and challenge.

**Scenario 2: This little org stayed home.** Then you have Microsoft — the most transformational software company of the 20th century. This is the organization that created Excel™ spreadsheets, which is the passive technology that new project management software has to displace. You know what I am talking about. The de facto solution for everything — "we'll just use a spreadsheet." Basically, Excel transitioned from brand name to generic name like Kleenex and Band-Aid. Despite their transformational prowess of the late 1900s, they have lost their mojo. They missed the whole touch screen and tablet shift. They ignored the cloud revolution and yet they have the largest install base of any other technology. Microsoft had it, lost it, but has an incredible opportunity to regain its innovative edge by aligning with market changes and demand and leveraging its credibility and install base. Perhaps Microsoft 360 and new CEO Satya Nadella will lead the comeback by adapting to change.

**Scenario 3: This little org had roast beef, but may now have none.** *Bless its heart*, Kodak® was a camera pioneer. It enabled us to capture some the most important moments of our lives, all on film. Film was its own downfall. Ironically, Kodak's research lab invented a digital camera in 1975, but the organization never pursued it. The company white-knuckled the almighty film so much that it crushed its future. During its bankruptcy woes in 2013, the famed imaging company had to sell off more than $525 million worth of patents, which were scooped up for a steal from major unseen competitors like Apple™ and Google™. Had it, lost it, and may never recover among all the Smartphone and technology competitors.

Let this story of the *three little orgs* be a beacon to steer your landing for the right organization.

Clearly defining only three categories of organizations is an oversimplification. Organizations are immensely complex. Organizations are made of multiple functions, departments, and people. Be careful to avoid making snap judgments. In the heat of the moment, your emotions may take over like the Hulk does Bruce Banner, and you may miss some promising signals.

Now it's time to be curious.

- *How do you know if you are part of a hierarchical innovation crusher vs. a flat, nimble innovation powerhouse?*
- *Or is your organization in transition and temporarily pausing a 'wild west' of innovation?*

## Actions speak louder than words.

Ten Actions of Innovative Organizations that you should be on the lookout for as you assess the viability of leadovation:

1. **Displays a Market-Driven, Evolving, Relevant Strategy.** Does your organization have a track record of change and evolving strategy? In this hyper-speed environment of today, it is imperative for organizations to adapt to and with the market and customer needs. If your organization has been holding on to its dying cash cow, with no track record of change, then it is probably one of the lucky ones that caught a passing trend and will go away like the Dodo.

   The most sustainable and innovative companies are the ones that see far enough down the road to change lanes *before* the crash. Take IBM for example. They started as a mainframe computer manufacturer in 1911, and today they are a one of the largest technology-enabling consulting firms.

   If reinvention is not the cornerstone of your organization, you may need to *exit stage left*. One thing is for sure, you

   "The momentum of all those wheels is too great for one person's passionate will."

cannot change an organization by yourself, no matter how genius you are. The momentum of all those wheels is too great for one person's passionate will.

2. **Ranks as Market Leader, or at Least Top Five.** External validation is often an indicator of reality. Although with the unicorn hype of today, you may start to wonder if the journalists, pundits, and market watchdogs have lost their minds.

    In the end, profitability and cash flow will always reveal the truth. Therefore, if your company is ranked in the top five or so in its category, you can safely say it has delivered at least some level of innovation.

    Just look at the top 10 companies on the Fortune 500 survivor list from 1955, while many have been bought or changed their names, they were all market leaders over and over: General Motors, Exxon Mobil, US Steel, General Electric, Esmark, now owned by Conagra, Chrysler, now owned by Daimler-Benz, Armour, now owned by Henkel, Gulf Oil, branded as Chevron in the 80s, now a network of alliances called Gulf Oil Limited Partnership, Mobil, now ExxonMobil, and DuPont[12]. All of these survivors are market leaders. They have a proven track record of change and innovation and therefore, value, as proven by all the ownership and name changes.[13]

    It's not just Fortune 500, but also Inc 500, and Fast Company's Top 100. Just look at any of the major media list for top companies and see for yourself the ones that hold market leader positions.

    Innovators are always leaders, regardless if we are referring to people or organizations. If your organization has fallen behind, then you may have been lucky or you may just be in transition.

    Look at the organization's three to five year strategy; *does it match the trends of digitization, globalization or customer-centric mentality?* If so, then you probably are in an organization that will foster innovation from within.

3. **Executes.** Riding the coattails of number two *(Ranks as Market Leader, or at Least Top Five)*, organizations that have secured market leader positions are known for execution. They deliver.

---

[12] *These companies all have US registered trademarks: IBM, General Motors, Exxon Mobil, US Steel, General Electric, Esmark, Conagra, Chrysler, Daimler-Benz, Armour, Henkel, Gulf Oil, Chevron in the 80's, Mobil, Exxonmobil, DuPont.*

[13] *http://fortune.com/2014/06/02/first-fortune-500/*

It is impossible to have a healthy balance sheet without executing. These organizations aren't like the great Greek philosophers of ancient times, philosophizing about grandeur and circumstance. No way. These organizations "just do it." Nike® would be proud.

And sometimes they make mistakes in execution. Let's face it, no one is a fortuneteller and sometimes past success can blind executives when making decisions. Executives and companies miss the mark on occasion and that is ok, if handled correctly. Take Netflix™ for example. In 2011, when CEO Reed Hastings decided to spin out their DVD service and raise the price of Netflix, disaster ensued. Netflix lost more than 800,000 customers and its stock price dropped 77% almost overnight. Many of the seasoned management team exited. As for Hastings, he instantly fell from grace, going from Fortune's "businessperson of the year," to a common satirical theme on *Saturday Night Live*. His arrogance, poor communication with customers, and relentless pursuit of online streaming raked the company over the coals. The only way he could dig out was to face the music, admit he was wrong, and roll back changes customers demanded. In hindsight, we see that his vision was dead on, but his lack of collaboration with his fellow executives, employees, and customers almost ended it all. He did execute, but it turned out to be an almost solo, kamikaze-like mission. Netflix did recover. Today Netflix has about a $40 billion market cap and leads the digital entertainment streaming industry hands down. Lesson for us all: *blind execution without collaborating with employees and customers may lead to epic failure.*

Ask yourself:

|  | <ul><li>*Does your organization execute?*</li><li>*Do leaders work with employees and customers to vet radical changes in strategy?*</li><li>*Are competitors, big or small, eating you for lunch as your organization lies unresponsive?*</li></ul> |
| --- | --- |

4. **Embodies an Environment of Trust.** One of the hardest things to gain and easiest things to lose: Trust. Trust is the bedrock of innovation and change.

*Remember our addiction to risk mitigation and certainty*? Trust is the only way to combat the big "F" word, Fear. Fear of failure is the number one reason why people and organizations don't change or innovate. Many leaders talk about it. They even send managers and employees to failure camps and conferences to increase their comfort with fear, but too often those are just superficial actions. It is natural for everyone to be risk averse. No one wants to fail. But failure is a part of discovery.

The only tangible way to overcome this anthropological need is to *reframe the idea of failure*. Scientists have done this for years, by looking at failure in experimentation as the process of learning. It's the simple process of elimination. If you can eliminate a possibility when proven unsuccessful, you now have increased your chances of finding the right solution.

- *Does your organization create a safe place to fail?*
- *Does it allow anyone to object or share his/her opinion without consequences?*

If you get that twinge in your gut before you suggest something new or execute a small pilot to test a new process or service, then you may be in an organization that isn't well suited for innovation. However, be sure you aren't projecting your own fear on the situation. Take a common tactic from meteorologists and send a test balloon and see how the organization reacts. If your well-intentioned trial balloon fails and you get ostracized, demoted, and publicly humiliated, then you know you are in the wrong place.

5. **Aligns Performance Measures and Reward Systems for Innovation and Teams.** People do what they are incentivized to do. That is law; written in stone. It doesn't always mean money. It can mean incentives, which could range from bragging rights, confidence, portfolio projects, and perhaps cash and prizes.

If your organization has a track record of rewarding self-promoting buzz-word parrots, then you are in the wrong place. Some organizations suffer from what I call the "Shiny-Ball Syndrome." Some symptoms include: praising or promoting individuals for parroting Internet buzzwords when no one knows what they really mean; resourcing empty projects to appear innovative; or letting the idea guy keep pitching ideas, but do nothing. This is organizational ADD fueled by the hope of instant success without any messy, painful, hard work. It never works. It builds resentment and disengagement.

If your organization has innovation in its veins, it will align its performance metrics with rapid trial innovation, quick failures, institutional learning from those failures, and teamwork. It takes a team to innovate, not a lone genius. That term is a cliché for a reason.

As a leader, you often have control within your team to align those metrics to the desired collaborative behavior. Be brave and institute reward systems for teams, NOT individuals. Don't give out a trophy for skinned knees, but for real trial efforts of teams who buck the status quo and make the organization better. You have the power within your reach; all you have to do is take it.

6. **Communicates Clearly and Transparently the Strategic Direction and Execution Expectations.** It's ironic that communication is the leading cause of failure. It's something we learn our whole lives to do and yet, repeatedly, organizations and individuals fail to clearly communicate strategy and direction.

   I'm not talking about that mission statement that is collecting dust or posted on a faded poster in the break room. That is not communicating. Stop kidding yourself. The communication box is NOT checked.

   Misinformation and misinterpretation are innovation killers. If your organization is hiding behind 50-cent words instead of simply communicating and sharing information across the ranks of your organization, then get out. As the outside environment creates more ambiguity, it will be even more critical for you to communicate and re-communicate, up, down, and around as dynamics change.

   Employees want to help the company succeed. Keeping them in the dark not only confuses them, but also disenchants them of their ability to make an impact. In order to leverage your talent effectively, they must know the company strategic direction, why the company can deliver that strategy, and what their role is in making that happen. It is the only way to align, focus, and activate to win. If this notion is foreign to the culture of your organization, you may be in a "hierarchical innovation crusher."

7. **Encourages Autonomy.** Freedom is a powerful motivator. Freedom to figure out a working solution, a product roll out, or just tweak an internal communication process, is the path to less middle school complaining and more productive, innovative adult output.

Watch out for organizations that hide their information, processes, or systems. It is a sure sign they are crushers. That need for control will always lead to bad decisions and the market will respond. Those organizations often spend millions, if not more, to develop a product, never asking a single customer's input, and they will fail. Eventually that money and their position will fade with that behavior.

Let me be clear, I am not saying your organization should go all hippy-dippy and let your teams go wild. It's actually simple in theory: Clearly communicate the measureable goal, strategic direction, and set up an iterative feedback process. Then get the hell out of their way and let them work. Channel your Eric Carmen or Celine Dion and let them work "All By Myself [Themselves]" with frequent check ins and earnest experienced counsel.

- *Does your organization promote autonomy at every level of the organization?*
- *Are there clear goals, milestone parameters and coaching feedback processes?*

If so, you might be in a nimble innovation powerhouse. Woot!

8. **Demonstrates Flexibility.** This attribute is loaded. Flexibility comes in all types. From flexible work arrangements, including remote working or nontraditional work hours, to project shares and job mobility.

In 2013, this notion of a flexible, mobile workforce was brought into question, when Yahoo!® CEO Marissa Mayer shutdown the telecommuter policy at Yahoo! and gave remote workers an option — come in or get out. The official memo used the need for collaboration and speed as the drivers of the policy, but was that just business save-your-ass jargon? Insiders and analysts alike had their perspectives. There were debates on both sides of the issue.

- *Was this a mechanism of totalitarian control?*
- *Or was it a way to evaluate the core, revenue-generating activities of a fledgling company and leverage the full power of a nimble collaborative workforce?*

The debate still continues, and the data does support some flexible work arrangements as a driver of innovation and talent. A Gallup State of the American Workplace report[14] found that people who work remotely are more engaged, enthusiastic, and committed to their work — but only if they work outside the office 20% of the time or less. Just like all things, too much of anything will prove to be counterproductive, but in the world of progressive, digitally fluent era, some flexibility is necessary for progress.

- *Is fluidity a central tenet of your organization?*
- *Or does your organization freak out when employees want to work for other managers or try something new?*

9. **Rocks the Confidence.** The tone and behavior of executives and the overall culture of the organization define an organization's confidence. The litmus test of a confident organization is in the way they react when they lose.

- *Are they bashing your competition publically when outmaneuvered during a market transition?*
- *Are the executives scrambling for self-protection and blaming individuals or business units for the failure?*
- *Are they poised and professional, owning up to a mistake or a surprise and then reacting with swift action to get back into the game?*

Don't misinterpret confidence with arrogance. Ensure that the culture of your organization isn't showing signs of complacency and entitlement. That is a red flag.

- *Do the leaders in your organization display confidence in the organization's direction? In its management team? In its employees and employee decisions?*
- *How have they reacted in the past to a loss?*

---

[14] *http://www.gallup.com/services/178514/state-american-workplace.aspx*

Similar to trust, confidence is a key ingredient to innovation and change. Without it, no one will take risks.

10. **Promotes Real Innovation Efforts** — Successes and Failures.

- *Does your organization promote innovation efforts no matter how large or small? What about both successes and failures?*
- *Do they promote real impactful change, not just parroting insignificant efforts?*
- *Do they have a healthy attitude around experimentation and learning?*

Here is an example of a company that embraces failures and successes and incorporates them both into a formal, disciplined feedback process. Pixar,® often referred to as the most successful creative enterprise, has openly shared its approach to failure and creative evolution process. Founder Ed Catmull explains that comparing an early idea to a finished product is a death move for creativity. He refers to the first few iterations of a character or story as "ugly babies." It is up to the team to whole-heartedly turn that baby into a beauty. Everyone openly embraces starting points that some would view as failures and the evolutionary success from a massive team effort. This approach certainly works, since Pixar has earned 15 Academy Awards, averages $600 million a film, and all but one movie is listed within the Top 50 Highest Grossing Animated Movies.

*How does your organization stack up to this hot list of actions?* You should assess to find out. Unfortunately, no matter the herculean effort you person-ally make, an organization is like a machine. Once the wheels and mechan-ics are in motion, it is almost impossible to change or stop them. Instead of wasting your energy, work at a company that will embrace your passion and vision for innovation. Leadovators need a nurturing environment to operationalize change and deliver innovation continuously at speed. You should optimize your energy and effort at a place that will serve you, your employees, and ultimately the market and its customers in this *Innovation Revolution*. Assess, rally, or let go and move on.

*Which organization do you work for?*

- Nimble Innovation Powerhouse (innovative and wants to continue to grow).

- Innovation Comeback Kid (had innovation, lost it, can make a comeback).
- Hierarchical Innovation Crusher (got lucky, but can't innovate or survive moving forward).

You can take a quick 10 question Three Little Orgs Assessment[15] to determine where your organization falls by visiting http://tinyurl.com/threelittleorgs.

After you assess which of the *Three Little Orgs* you are a part of, here are your next actions to put you in the right place.

If you are working in the organization that got lucky, but can't innovate or survive in the future, there is a big move to make.

## Three Top Actions, if innovation or survival is not possible:

1. Create and execute an exit strategy.
2. Use the Three Little Orgs Assessment to create a preferred organization list and start working your exit plan to find a new position where you are poised for innovative success.
3. Update your LinkedIn profile, pimp out your resume and start hitting up your network for opportunities.

If you are working for the organization that was innovative and lost it, but can still make a comeback, this is your chance to shine. It won't be easy, but you may very well be this place's big hope. With your newfound Leadovator skills and knowledge of what it takes to be an innovative company, this is your chance to make a huge impact on the transition. You will have to channel your inner CIA secret agent combined with your best politician.

## Three top Actions, to lead the transition comeback:

1. Identify what are the weakest areas of your organization. *What have you lost? What is the market saying about your offerings?*
2. Investigate and pinpoint your leaks. Look at the last two years of data around customer attrition and sales deal loss. You will see patterns of a greater issue. Find which one is within your team's purview, and solve it.

---

[15] *http://tinyurl.com/threelittleorgs*

3.  Share your findings of the innovation weak points and customer attrition with your peer colleagues across as many functions as you can. Try to inspire them to be a part of an *Innovation Revolution* to solve at least one of the identified weak points. Together y'all *can* transform.

Boom! You are now positioned as a collaborative leader who delivers. If you can create a groundswell of support and action, you can accelerate the comeback.

If you are in an organization that has innovation and wants to continue to grow it, you are in the catbird seat, as they say. You have the infrastructure and culture to accelerate innovation. The pressure is on for you to manage your employees to adapt and deliver repeatedly.

## Three Top Actions, to continue to grow:

1.  Identify if there are any at-risk areas from the assessment. Leading companies sometimes fall in the blind trap and lose site of the horizon. If you find one, ask yourself how you can shore up the position. Make it happen.

2.  Push your team to go beyond their current success. Challenge them to co-create at least one new customer value project semi-annually. Support their efforts through resources and barrier removal.

3.  Cross the aisle to other functions and bring them in on your innovative efforts. Perhaps this cooperation is not explicit in your annual goals, but it demonstrates your visionary prowess. You must lead by example. Find one other function you naturally can partner with and buddy up with the leader and team. Collaborate on one key performance indicator and showcase your success to the rest of the organization.

Don't be paranoid that your organization is going to lose it. Just always remember change is guaranteed and only the nimble will survive.

# THE Weekly ZING

## Your Innovation Challenge
## Switcharoo

Right-hand dominant?

For one hour pick up everything with your left.
Lefties, do the reverse.

Changing your approach is half the battle.

Share your insights with @48Innovate use
#switcharoo.

# Chapter 5

# The Answers You Seek Are Within

*"If the rate of change on the outside exceeds the rate of change
on the inside, the end is near."*

*— Jack Welch*

Promise of the Chapter:

- Review the origins of systemic control hindering innovation in the enterprise.
- Define your secret weapon hiding in plain sight — INTRApreneurs.
- Offer enabling strategies to empower your INTRApreneurs to evolve the organization from the inside out.

Get your head out of the sand. You must face this accelerated, disruptive era with courage and vision. No more denying where your focus must be: INSIDE. Inside yourself, inside your organization, and inside out. Ironically, your internal operations, structure, and people are within your control, and yet you continue to seek external Band Aids, instead of transforming your core to deliver innovation systematically. Scotty from the Starship Enterprise, keeps yelling, "She's not going to hold," and you keep saying, "Give it all we got." Eventually you are going to run out of "it" — energy, talent, market share, competitive advantage, momentum unless something changes.

- *How to re-engineer the "it" so it will hold under fire in the great unknown? More importantly, how can you re-engineer the "it" to deliver value-creating innovation, with shrinking and over-extended resources amid massive information, complexities and pressure, systematically and at speed?*
- *How to lead The Innovation Revolution?*

Activate your inner Leadovator.

- You must let go of the way things have always been done.
- You must bravely face fear, failure, and frustration and lean forward.
- You must identify, recruit, and empower an army of entrepreneurial-minded employees, called INTRApreneurs, and provide them a scalable, repeatable method to deliver innovation consistently.

You read that right, INTRApreneurship is making a comeback from the 1980s, and it's your secret weapon to deliver innovation and impact systematically and at speed.

Here is why:

- Those millennials and Gen Fluxers who are demanding autonomy, ownership, and meaning are natural-born INTRApreneurs, who already speak digital and thrive on disruption and uncertainty.
- Startups aren't the only ones that get to benefit from the era of entrepreneurship — the enterprise has the cash flow, the credibility and the customers — all that stands in the way now is a shift in mindset and method.
- Leaders will be defined by the brave choice to operationalize change among a headwind of doubt and dysfunction.

Truth is, INTRApreneurship isn't a new concept. It was made famous by one of the most influential CEOs and leaders of the late 1900s, former GE CEO Jack Welch, who through his simplifying and empowering actions, increased market value from $12 billion in 1981 to $280 billion, making 600 acquisitions while shifting into emerging markets.

This concept was first introduced in the 1980s by Gifford Pinchot, author of the international best-selling book INTRApreneuring: *Why You Don't Have to Leave the*

**INTRAPRENEUR**

noun in·tra·pre·neur \, in-trə-prə-ˈnər, -ˈnùr, -ˈnyùr\

DEFINITION of an intrapreneur: a person in a large corporation empowered to create new products without being constrained by standard procedures.

*Corporation to Become an Entrepreneur*. Pinchot defined an INTRApreneur as a person in a large corporation, empowered to create new products without being constrained by standard procedures.

*So what does INTRApreneurship have to do with leading systemic innovation?*

- It's the cultural foundation needed to transform those dysfunctional internal operations into a nimble, adaptive ecosystem to deliver consistent innovation at speed.
- It's the only way to compete with those pesky startups and harness the power of entrepreneurship on the inside.
- It's the only way you will recruit and retain top talent including the millennials and Gen Fluxers, to sustain your competitive advantage.
- It's the key to dominating the new normal and successfully future-proof your organization by operationalizing change.

"Reunited and it feels so good." A comparison of the business trends of then and now reveals why it's time to re-embrace INTRApreneurship as a strategic management practice to accelerate innovation, growth, profits, and sustainability for the future.

| Business Trends of 1980s – 2000 | Business Trends of 2000 – Today |
| --- | --- |
| Total Quality Management | Lean Startup Movement and Stampede of Unicorns |
| Waterfall or Stage-Gate Product Development | Open Source, Digitization and the rise of Internet of Things or IOT |
| Focus on Strategy Management and Rise of Big 5 Consulting Firms | Employee demographic transforming to millennials and Gen Fluxers |

In the 1980s until about the 2000s, before the bursting of the big tech bubble, there was the introduction of Total Quality Management, which was a structured process of quality improvement through feedback and development. On the heels of that movement was what we refer to as the "waterfall" product development process where one has to go through a series of gates and approvals to release. At the same time there was a huge demand for strategy consulting, which lead to the Big 5 consulting firms: Accenture, Deloitte, Ernst & Young, KPMG and PriceWaterhouseCoopers. The assumption, at the time, was that through corporate controls and strategy, execution would follow. Sometimes it worked, but looking back, it actually created the bureaucratic mess satirized by Dilbert, "The Office" and "Office Space" that is holding your organization back. No matter what anyone says, execution is the most common failure point for organizations.

Juxtapose that business environment against today's hyper-change environment, where it's cheaper to start a company than buy a new car. The introduction of the Lean Startup Movement and more than 140 $1 billion dollar-valuation startups, popularly named unicorns, exemplifies a much different environment than before. Many of these disruptive startups have capitalized on connecting anything and everything due to the open source and digitization era, which offers access to almost unlimited data, technology, and customers. Then you have the emerging next phase of this era called the Internet of Things (IOT) — enabling the connection of almost everything. Add that to a transformational change in values of work and expectation of meaning and ownership from the rising Generation Flux and millennial workforce, 70% of whom expect to work for themselves or independently in the future rather than being employed within a traditional organizational structure.[16] Sharing, connectivity, infinite access, and independence create the necessity for larger corporations to evolve to a more open and INTRApreneurial model.

What that means for you as a Leadovator is to understand how INTRAprenuership can help you lead *The Innovation Revolution* in the enterprise to meet the speeding, shifting demands of today. More importantly, it requires you to let go of the systemic command and control and create a new systemic method that empowers and engages your workforce to make confident, meaningful decisions that result in impact. You must transform from within, which includes perception, people, and processes. As cheesy as it sounds, you can't lead a movement unless you have followers, and in this pursuit, you need to enable mini-me leaders called INTRApreneurs. You know who I am talking about — those aggressive, persistent, challenging, risk-taking, idea-pitching, brilliant, sometimes annoying employees within your organization.

---

[16] *2014 The Deloitte Millennial Survey: https://www2.deloitte.com/al/en/pages/about-deloitte/articles/2014-millennial-survey-positive-impact.html*

These INTRApreneurs are essential to operationalize innovation at speed in order to deliver sustained value and competitive advantage.

These employees intrinsically want to make an impact. They hold all the information and experience to explore new markets, create new solutions, and innovate from within, but it is up to leaders to unearth the creative and lucrative potential of their talent. Your employees are the ones who interact with your customers every day. They are the ones that fend off your competitors every day, AND, they are the ones that know and work in your organizational culture every single day.

*Yearning for the exciting world of entrepreneurship?* Yearn no more. INTRApreneurs are your gateway into entrepreneurship inside the enterprise. INTRApreneur employees act and react just like entrepreneurs. Luckily for you, they need you as much as you need them. INTRApreneurs need an organization, a structure, and a steady paycheck, which prevents their exit to launch a startup that might just nip at your heels.

An INTRApreneur is an employee who is both willing and able to develop and implement innovative solutions, often independently or with a small team, and who creates exponential impact to an organization. If your organization is the platform to operationalizing innovation, INTRApreneurs are your innovative results engine, and you are the conductor.

You don't need a Myers Briggs® test or any other traditional talent-personality-strength-weakness-assessment to identify these INTRApreneurs.

**Ten Telltale Signs Your Employee is an INTRApreneur:**

1. Trouble-maker — more likely to ask for forgiveness than permission.
2. Risk-taker and uber resilient.
3. Problem solver.
4. Adaptable and thrives in reinvention.
5. Sees opportunity in everything.
6. Inquisitive — constantly asking why and tinkering.
7. Intense and passionate — work hard, play hard.
8. Competitive.
9. Self-starter, independent worker.
10. Craves flexibility, variety and spontaneity.

You may be asking yourself, if these INTRApreneurs are so awesome, then what prevents them from leaving an organization, starting their own company and becoming an entrepreneur? That's where the difference between INTRApreneur and entrepreneur comes into play. INTRApreneurs have too much to lose to take the enormous risk of leaving it all to start a company that has a 90% chance of failure.

*What are examples of that "too much to lose" for an INTRApreneur?* It could be a mortgage, family to support, or big college debt. There is usually some sort of financial reason that keeps them in check.

The truth of the matter is ... INTRApreneurs do better with structure. An organization is a structured working environment. Because INTRApreneurs are fast, creative beings, they tend to pinball around. The structure of an organization keeps them in the bounds of productivity.

Finally, INTRApreneurs are craftsmen, artisans of a sort. They are amazing at their craft or skill. They don't want to master all the functions of an organization. If they are marketing geniuses, they don't want to have to deal with accounting or the credibility and accuracy of balance sheets and profit and loss filings.

These employees are your best resource to operationalize innovation, but they don't come without their challenges. For most people, their greatest strength tends to be their greatest weakness. These INTRApreneurs are no different, except for maybe the intensity of the swing between productive and neurotic.

**Three Enabler Strategies, to help manage three big challenges on your quest to ushering systematic innovation and lead *The Innovation Revolution* for your organization:**

1. **Creators, not Maintainers.** INTRApreneurs are natural creators. The act of creating drives these employees. It doesn't matter if it is a product or process. But once that project has been tested, launched and running, that is when an INTRApreneur wants to bail. They do not do maintenance. You should know this important tendency when building a team. You need a balance of talent and a good strategy to manage this behavior. The best way to do this is to couple a junior or less experienced employee with an INTRApreneur. It's a perfect talent management strategy. Wicked creative self-starter to create, test and launch matched with

an eager junior sponge to learn and develop while adding tons of value. And if you are lucky, you will follow that transition with a technology automation to scale and reallocate to the next big innovation.

I am sure you are saying to yourself, why on earth do I have to accommodate this project ADD. It's like most things: you can be frustrated and try to force someone to do what you think is expected, or you can accept the situation and manage it to your advantage. And advantage it is, these INTRApreneurs are the ones you will allow to make key decisions that would ordinarily be backlogged in your inbox. As a Leadovator, you must constantly empower more people within the enterprise to make more decisions and take more impactful actions. In today's complex, hyper-drive environment, there is not enough time or brainpower for you to do it all. Everything is shifting rapidly, so in order to keep pace, you must empower, engage, and let go to operationalize innovation.

2. **Prone to Burn Out.** INTRApreneurs are like a match. You light them up and they explode with genius, passion, and productivity. But that burst comes at a big price. Poof. And just like that, their fire is out. At first this will drive you nuts, but that is because you have the mindset of this linear nine to five, Monday to Friday work routine. If you open your mind to different work models, not only will you be less frustrated, you will also maximize the output of your employees. Give your INTRApreneurs multiple projects with varying deadlines. This will allow them to self-manage their energy and productivity. When they get bored or burned out from one, they can reignite with the next one. You should also encourage your INTRApreneurs to take time to rest or do non-work experiences. This will not only help them sustain, but also inspire them in ways no one thought of. You know you have a backlog of projects awaiting attention. Pick three and communicate clearly the priority to avoid any misfiring or missed deadlines.

3. **Poisoned by Perfection.** We all know this one, regardless whether an employee is categorized as an *INTRApreneur*. Know the obsession with perfection is magnified in an INTRApreneur. The plight of a perfectionist is futile. There is no such thing, since the world around us is fluid and in constant flux. This is where your leadership experience kicks into gear. Your role as a coach comes into play. You have to show the INTRApreneur the logic around "good enough." You must demonstrate that exponential effort is not equal to the gains toward nonexistent perfection. If you define the "good enough" threshold for a project, you will better

manage an INTRApreneur's energy and frustration, while establishing continuous capacity to deliver again and again.

All of these challenges can be easily managed by building a trusting relationship with your INTRApreneur. It cannot be based on hierarchical power. Think of yourself more as a peer-coach relationship vs. a boss. The whole concept of boss conveys power and control. Most INTRApreneurs just need some grounding, context, and perspective. Their intentions are earnest. Remembering that fact will be essential for you to manage your expectations, frustrations, and productivity, while harnessing their entrepreneurial spirit, artisanal skill, and resilience on your quest to deliver innovation consistently at speed.

A 21st century Leadovator must inspire these INTRApreneurs to co-create and co-lead this new shift to revolutionize business-as-usual and deliver results among the complex disruptions. It's your only hope to successfully lead *The Innovation Revolution*.

# THE Weekly ZING

## Your Innovation Challenge
## Mileage Milestone

An innovative mind looks at things differently.

Practice this...next time you get in your car, look at your mileage.

Calculate how many miles you need to get to an interesting number that represents a cool date in history or an old phone number.

Make a mental note and see if you remember it when you pass that milestone.

Share your mileage milestone with @48Innovate use #mileagemilestone.

# Part 1

## Complete: 360° Reality Assessments

Now you know your starting position.

You acknowledge and understand trends disrupting business-as-usual at light speed.

You have evaluated yourself, your organization and your employees to inform your direction.

You have actively started observing and recognizing habits or processes that derail innovation and action within the enterprise.

You enthusiastically accept the Leadovator challenge and dare to thwart dysfunctional internal bias and processes that perpetuate siloed, spot-innovation efforts in service of leading *The Innovation Revolution* — a movement toward systemic innovation inside the enterprise, powered by INTRApreneurs.

Ready to discover how to lead this *Innovation Revolution*?

**Next up:**

**Discover a new, employee-driven innovation method that works called Smart Speed.**™

Before the next page turn, you must prepare for a mind shift.

Stand up and do five cross kicks.

- CROSS KICKS -

Scientists have discovered this small physical action helps your brain change your perspective. The human brain has two hemispheres, each differing from the other. This is called hemispheric *lateralization*. Basically, people are either right- or left-handed; right- or left-brained. In order to shift your normal dominant response, you must activate the other side. This exercise stimulates both sides of the brain and physically prepares you for a new perspective.

# Part 2

# Smart Speed: A Mindset, A Method, and A Movement

Get out the corporate hazmat gear and put on your headlamp as we explore the corporate underbelly revealing top results and innovation killers lurking in your enterprise ... *the-what-should-not-be-named* behaviors and actions in your corporate culture and institutional norms that derail progress and change. These are those dysfunctional, often legacy internal processes that are hindering your ability to compete, and more importantly, drain your scarce resources and talent.

Then it's time for the big reveal. The Smart Speed Method that Leadovators need to lead *The Innovation Revolution*. You must stop driving innovation as a singular exercise and operationalize innovation continuously at speed. Smart Speed is a mindset, a method, a movement, all rolled into one. We will demonstrate how this INTRApreneurial system can eliminate waste, overcome institutional behaviors, and drive consistent innovative results in less time and money than traditional methods.

It's harsh. It's dirty. It's enlightening. It's inspiring. Prepare yourself for the truth that lies within and a field-tested method that delivers every time.

# Chapter 6

## The Corporate Underbelly — Unspoken Barriers to Systemic Innovation and Results

*"The truth does not change according to our ability to stomach it."*

*— Flannery O'Connor*

Promise of the Chapter:

- Highlight systemic misbehaviors that too often are ignored.
- Discover available resources to fuel *The Innovation Revolution*.
- Offer an actionable management manifesto to stop the madness.

### Not so AMAZing Work

In 2015, The New York Times wrote a scathing exposé on the most valuable retailer, worth an estimated $250 billion, Amazon. It's not the first time the media exposed harsh work conditions, but probably one of the first to highlight bad treatment of white collar workers.

The article highlighted the anxiety-provoking sessions called "business reviews," held weekly or monthly among various teams, where employees were quizzed on 50 – 60 pages of data. It revealed that the Anytime Feedback Tool was used to send scorching and scheming feedback about workers. It uncovered the practice of secret competitions, where different groups were given the same project without even knowing it, to see who could deliver better. And finally, managers who spend countless hours documenting paper trails to debate keeping high valued employees.[17]

---

[17] *http://www.fastcompany.com/3033093/work-smart/70-of-your-time-at-work-is-wasted-how-to-change-that*

The article notes most employees refused to allow the media outlet to reference them, which is probably why we don't see more articles highlighting the misuse of time and resources within companies. Amazon pays a big price for its relentless work culture with high turnover and burnout. Only time will reveal if this dog-eat-dog strategy will work for the long run. It does, however, demonstrate Business Guru Peter Drucker's famous quote: "Culture eats strategy for lunch."

Get ready for the naked truth. Your employees have become meeting mavens, email lobbers, slide slaves, Excel jockeys, and political animals. These innocuous activities seem harmless until you start adding them up and then hit them with a multiplier. Add in the demoralizing effect of this non-impactful yet required busywork, and you see how that could affect the bottom line. No wonder your best employees are headed for the door and willing to take less money for a different kind of work. I know it's a harsh truth. But truth it is.

The corporate world wastes so much valuable time and talent on busywork. In 2013, London Business School Strategy Professor Julian Birkinshaw published research revealing that on average employees spend 41% of their time on busy work. Some of the work is done by choice, i.e., it makes them feel as if they have accomplished something, and some forced by cultural norms, i.e., companies require a presentation for every discussion or several permutations of data spreadsheets.[18] Most managers complain they can't get resources when they need them, and it isn't for a lack of availability. Instead, it's the misallocation of those resources.

Let me share some real-live-no-jive cases to demonstrate the biggest productivity drains that are caused by corporate culture, norms, and expectations. These drains may seem harmless, but that is false. Your workforce is overworked and underappreciated. These business-as-usual norms are crushing their spirit, creativity, and sanity. And your future workforce will be made up of millennials and Gen Fluxers who will quit before they endure this dysfunction, leaving you farther behind. In order for you to lead *The Innovation Revolution*, the transformation to innovation as a daily operation, you must get rid of the busy-work requirements that emerged when there were lots more people resources and less advanced collaboration

---

[18] *https://hbr.org/2013/09/make-time-for-the-work-that-matters*

tools. By removing these legacy behaviors, you will unleash hidden productivity, motivation, and innovative thinking required to develop institutional innovation, adapt at speed, and deliver results consistently.

**Meetings.** There are 25 million meetings every day in the US, wasting more than $37 billion a year. Organizations collectively spend 15% of their time in meetings. WOW! And it gets worse the bigger your title. Middle management spends 35% of its time in meetings; upper management 50%. *What's that you say? You have to meet to get work done?* Absolutely, but management considers 67% of those meetings a failure.

These meetings fail due to a lack of purpose, meeting structure, the wrong participants, and the proliferation of multi-tasking, which 92% of employees admit they do during the meetings. The future looks grim with the flattening of organizational structures and more geographically dispersed teams where many leaders are thrust into more meetings to make decisions and become a bottleneck of progress. More depressing is the fact that 80% of virtual attendees are actively disengaged in the conversation, causing additional delays and increased adoption costs.[19] Meeting-Mavens-R-Us has become a core competency in organizations.

**Email.** Most employees, even all the way up the chain to CEO, spend 30-40% of their time on email, the majority which is internal.[20] *When is the last time you heard an internal email was the reason for a killer deal being closed? Or the cause of that next big development aha?* Rarely, if ever.

An average employee processes about 304 emails a week, costing $5,100 to $7,100 in loss of productivity a year per employee.[21] That's the hard data.

---

[19] https://www.themuse.com/advice/how-much-time-do-we-spend-in-meetings-hint-its-scary

[20] http://www.fastcompany.com/3033093/work-smart/70-of-your-time-at-work-is-wasted-how-to-change-that

[21] https://www.atlassian.com/time-wasting-at-work-infographic

Now let's explore the interruption effects, where every time someone is distracted with an email, it takes them 20 minutes to get back to the initial task. In addition, another study revealed we lose ten IQ points from this distraction game of tennis — email lob, bam email back, refocus, work, etc., the cycle continues. Consider that employees check their email 36 times an hour, which is a hell of a lot of time, focus, and diminished intellectual capacity.[22] If your employees are email lobbers, beware of all the results you are losing from the back and forth.

**Presos, presentations, decks and slides.** Most large organizations can't communicate without a Powerpoint presentation. In fact, Microsoft estimated that there are more than 30 million presentations each day,[23] which is about 350 given every second around the world.[24] And all the permutations, before, during, and after add up to more waste, which some suggest is 1.125 million minutes annually.[25]

Regardless of where you sit in an organization, this is a top skill required to communicate. Part of this is a direct result of virtual work, but before Webex,™ GoToMeeting,™ and Skype™ were invented, this was still the case. The 1980s fad just won't die. If you want to discuss any project, everyone asks for your slideware.

We interviewed hundreds of big corporate employees, and while many were embarrassed to admit the amount of time they spent creating Powerpoint presentations, on average they said they spend 20-25% of their time creating slide decks. Whoa!

**Here is a scenario one interviewee shared:**

An executive wants a read out on our project and go-forward plan. We pull together the team to document and prepare for the presentation. The team spends collectively 40 hours in three days to create the baseline deck. Then it goes to the middle manager for review and feedback. It's sent back with extreme suggested changes with less than a day to go. One martyr volunteers to send out a request to each team member to adjust their slide and collect the changes and ushers the presentation back

[22] https://hbr.org/2014/07/the-cost-of-continuously-checking-email/

[23] http://www.newyorker.com/magazine/2001/05/28/absolute-powerpoint

[24] http://www.bloomberg.com/news/articles/2012-08-30/death-to-powerpoint

[25] http://midnightsky.com.au/2015/03/you-do-the-maths/

through the same review cycle. Then there is a "dress rehearsal" meeting to go over the presentation with more changes in slides and talking points. At this point, a team of four to seven members of varying levels, including the manager, have spent more than 100 hours on this one slide deck. The big meeting happens and only five of the slides are reviewed and then there are more changes to the slide deck after the executive meeting, adding on at least another 15 hours from the team. If you are following this word problem, that is a whopping 155 hours of work on one slide deck in a given week, to merely report progress or status of a project.

This slide spin up and down is constant. Could you imagine what kind of meaningful output could be created if people weren't wasting their time on that perfect bullet or that perfect graphic that is not likely to ever been seen? The corporate world is producing slide slaves. No one in an interview says, "I can't wait to do Powerpoint with my life." Granted, Powerpoint is a medium for communication, but this obsession with perfection for a 30-minute executive meeting is beyond absurd and wastes the most precious of resources — time and talent.

I can speak from personal experience here, too. When I went from a giant company to a small one, I tried to create an elegant slide deck, detailing my plan to present to my small team. It was a work of corporate art ... the builds, oh, the choreographed slide animations.

Here is what happened when I revealed my fine Powerpoint art. First of all, they gave me the *crazy* look, then they said, "Ok, what else do you have?" I was left with that emperor-has-no-clothes feeling. I had been trained that this was the opening shot across the bow. This was the first step in buy-in and discussion. This nimble team said, "They paid you for this" (in a polite way, remember I live in the South). You see, they had already done a million more must-haves in the time it took for me to create a canvas of recommendations. Lesson learned: I never created another Powerpoint deck after that. Instead I asked questions via IM or picked up the phone. I confidently executed while collecting feedback along the way. It was a lesson I share with you. Those slide-slaves design amazing or not-so-amazing presentations that rarely generate revenue or exponential value. And in this agile world, it is a definite results killer.

**Spreadsheets**. Some estimate 10-30% of employees' time is spent creating, manipulating, and maintaining spreadsheets, costing an estimated $450 million a year.[26] It's spreadsheet mania in big organizations. This trend isn't a byproduct of the big data era. No, this is a legacy habit. Leaders unfortunately are stuck in these cells of hell every day. Pivot tables, data graphs, and ghetto business models are where they spend most of their time. Employees who are masterful spreadsheet jockeys can win favor with leaders up the stack, by helping them produce the data story to match their initiative or plan.

Spreadsheets aren't just for data manipulation, oh no. It is *the* defacto project management software, customer relationship management system, contact database, and editorial calendar. Employees report spending more than 20 hours on spreadsheets each week, though they asked not to be named.

Holy cow, if you add up the time spent in these top time-suck worm holes in a given week, that's up to 55% of the available time to do work, meaning most employees only spend 45% of their time doing meaningful work.[27] Again, I repeat, no one ever said they wanted to be a meeting maven, email lobber, slide slave, or spreadsheet jockey when they grow up, but that's what the corporate world is producing. No wonder managers and employees alike are struggling to get real work done.

This busywork is killing the bottom line and leaders are responsible. How can employees be creative and action-oriented if they are stuck wasting time in meetings, on email, tweaking slides or spreadsheets? These are the dysfunctional internal processes you, as a Leadovator, must eliminate. You want more resources and can't hire? Your answer is reallocating that busy work to meaningful, impactful work. Top talent will be beating down the door to get in to make a difference. Bring on the headline.

# INSERT YOUR COMPANY

Named Top Workplace Destination of Millennials

## GEN FLUXERS AND GLOBAL GENIUS TALENT

---

[26] *https://robertkugel.ventanaresearch.com/2013/03/01/spreadsheet-denial-is-a-big-issue/*
[27] *http://www.theatlantic.com/business/archive/2014/12/the-wasted-workday/383380/*

And let's reveal the worst time suck of all in the corporate world — **the politics**. Everyone complains about it; no one wants to play, but is it a total necessary evil. A 2012 survey by Robert Half International shows 56% of workers feel politicking is necessary to get ahead in their career.[28] Any time you have more than one person in a room, physical or virtual, there is a political play opportunity and that is not creating the trusting environment required for systemic innovation.

Hours are spent in side-bar conversations, extended lunch sessions, and IM conversations, figuring out how to position — oneself, one's project, team, or department. This is a learned behavior from management. There is always the usual boilerplate statement, *we don't engage in politics in this company*, and five minutes later someone asks how can we position this or that.

The corporate world has trained political animals. If they were unleashed in Washington, DC, watch out. The world may not recover. Credit taking, slide stealing, and bus-throwing actions are so common in big corporate, you always need to watch your back. It's a lot like an episode of *Orange is the New Black*. Watch out for that spreadsheet shank. More time is wasted on plotting than producing. Part of this is a result of the hierarchical set up and the outdated reward systems of promotion and advancement. Some of it is because in a large organization, it is easier to hide and stall. You see, it's easy to blame the usual suspects, like a project was delayed because of another group or a leader's lack of decision making. It's so pervasive that no one really knows what is real and what is made up. *And since most knowledge workers do their work in their head, how can you really measure it or manage it?*

All these behaviors are developing unproductive skills in your employees.

- *If your team were given a test today, would they crush the meeting, email, slideware, spreadsheet, and politics section?*
- *Is that leading to meaningful, relevant competitive advantage or results?*
- *Is that why when someone suggests something new, everyone clamors to be the first one to sink the idea?*

These are the biggest productivity busters and result killers driven by the organizational culture and expectations. If you want to discover untapped

---

[28] http://rhfa.mediaroom.com/office-politics

resources, you must start by changing expectations and thwarting these time-sucks in their tracks. It is impossible to usher systemic innovation into the enterprise with these behaviors.

Ok, after you pick your ego off the floor, are you ready for a solution to these corporate monsters and wasted talent? Do you dare to put that Leadovator title to work?

You must stop ignoring these drains on the enterprise in order to lead *The Innovation Revolution*.

**Here is your new management manifesto to stop the madness:**

1. **Set a meeting limit for the week.** No more than X meetings in a given week. When the team hits the quota, decline every request. Give your employees permission to do the same and back them up if they get push back from ANYONE.

2. **Decline any meeting** that doesn't have a focused outcome and agenda.

3. Give your team permission to **stop responding to an email chain after two replies.** Suggest they pick up the phone to discuss the message and establish next steps.

# TENETS OF THE MANAGEMENT MANIFESTO

## SET A MEETING LIMIT FOR THE WEEK

DECLINE ANY MEETING THAT DOESN'T HAVE A FOCUSED OUTCOME AND AGENDA | **GIVE** YOUR TEAM **PERMISSION**

## IMPOSE A SLIDE LIMIT

**PROVIDE** A TIME AND SAFE PLACE TO VENT FRUSTRATIONS | IF THEY DON'T HAVE **INFINITE SLIDES,** THEY WON'T SPEND INFINITE TIME PERFECTING THEM

4. **Impose a slide limit.** If they don't have infinite slides, they won't spend infinite time perfecting them. The same can be applied to data analysis and spreadsheet permutations.

5. **Provide a time and safe place to vent frustrations**, but limit it to that time. I hosted a monthly "Bitchin' Chicken Session" at the local fried chicken joint called Bojangles™ so the team could vent, but knew in meetings we were going to discuss innovative solutions and support all members of the team.

It's hard setting the example, just ask your Mama. The only way to stop this nonsense is, well, to stop doing it. You are the key to more productive and meaningful work. Be brave. You are a Leadovator now!

# THE Weekly ZING

## Your Innovation Challenge
## BLOT

Email communication is a time suck. In your next email to your employee, try this communication trick.

**BLOT: Bottom Line On Top**
Think about how many emails people get today. Make it more likely they will read yours over others by putting the "ask," challenge, or win" first and then support it with information below. Set the example of effective email communication and watch the productivity roll in.

*Special thanks to UNC Kenan Flagler Business Professor, Tim Flood for this gem. Works every time.*

Share your insights with
@48Innovate use #BLOT.

# Chapter 7

## Buzzwords Gone Bad — How Empty Buzzwords Impede Action, Innovation, and Results

*"You keep using that word. I do not think it means what you think it means."*

— Inigo Montoya, Princess Bride

Promise of Chapter:

- Reveal the damage of miscommunication and misuse of buzzwords in your pursuit of systemic innovation.
- Offer tips to help you take the buzz out of buzzwords and clearly communicate among a constant flow of ambiguity.

In order to lead *The Innovation Revolution* and deliver systemic innovation in the enterprise, you must create an environment that is authentic and open. Innovation can't flourish with constant misinformation, misdirection, and misalignment. *Buzzwords gone bad* cause this mayhem. They are like a splinter. When left in place, they fester, which creates even more doubt and dysfunction. All your energy is wasted on digging out instead of leaping forward. Make room for innovation by getting rid of abused buzzwords and their aftermath.

One of the measurable effects of buzzword misuse is the cost of poor communication to businesses. Depending on which industry you investigate, the costs per year runs in the millions or billions. There are a variety of ways communication effectiveness is measured. Here is a sampling of the potential costs organizations face by using these innocent buzzwords.

**Chalk up a whopping $12 billion annually in the US healthcare system.** A 2010 study from the University of Maryland's Robert H. Smith School of Business, measured a titanic loss of $12 billion annually to the U.S. healthcare system, attributed in large measure to poor and inefficient communication among doctors, nurses, and other healthcare providers. A single 500-bed hospital, according to the research, suffers losses of over $4 million annually due to various communication inefficiencies.[29]

**Add $37 billion in losses to companies because of employee misunderstanding.** A 2008 white paper commissioned by employment assessment specialist Cognisco revealed annual losses of $37 billion from miscommunication. The study involving U.S. and UK companies attributed the loss to "actions taken by employees who have misunderstood or misinterpreted -- or were misinformed about or lack confidence in their understanding of -- company policies, business processes, job function or a combination of the three."[30]

**Toss in a 56% risk of failure for projects as a result of poor communication.** A recent study conducted by the Project Management Institute (PMI) revealed the negative impact of ineffective communication to project execution. Here are examples the study cited:

"Companies risk $135 million for every $1 billion spent on a project and new research indicates that $75 million of that $135 million (56 percent) is put at risk by ineffective communications, indicating a critical need for organizations to address communications deficiencies at the enterprise level."

"Ineffective communications is the primary contributor to project failure one third of the time, and had a negative impact on project success more than half the time."[31]

I am sure buzzwords didn't cause all that risk, loss of productivity or cash, but they are a huge source of miscommunication that destroys innovation.

Buzzwords are taking over. Like many things, these words never intended to wreak such havoc. They never asked to be abused, but unfortunately they are constantly misused, misdirected, and transformed into weapons of mass innovation destruction.

---

[29] http://www.rhsmith.umd.edu/news/us-hospitals-waste-12-billion-annually-because-poor-communication

[30] www.cognisco.com/countingthecost

[31] http://www.pmi.org/~/media/PDF/Business-Solutions/The-High-Cost-Low-Performance-The-Essential-Role-of- Communications.ashx

I know you are secretly nodding your head. You are either wearing a big fat grin of acknowledgement or a chagrin of embarrassment. It's ok. It's the reality we all live in.

What is the big deal? They are just words right? Who hasn't played a little innocent game of buzzword bingo in a meeting? How can you not laugh out loud or secretly snicker when you hear phrases like – "We must leverage synergetic partnerships and collaboration to capitalize on the paradigm shift from convergence to disruption to exponentially affect the bottom line." Words are powerful and the misuse is destructive. As a 21st century Leadovator, you must bust buzzwords gone bad to stamp out the pervasive misinformation, inaction, and internal dysfunction, to make room for inclusive and honest debate that leads to perpetual forward progress.

## Three Kinds of Buzzwords

1. **Industry jargon and acronyms.** These are the industry-specific jargon and acronyms that are created out of a need for speed and a common language. These are usually created naturally from common use in a corporate culture, community or function. Their intent is harmless, but often times the usage misguides and excludes.

2. **Classic corporate clichés.** Usually clichés begin as a metaphor to help explain complex concepts, but with time and overuse, their original intent gets lost. I'm sure when someone came up with "Don't boil the ocean," they never thought it would catch on and be used as a common phrase for don't try to do or solve too many things at once. In business, it seems we use clichés as a litmus test to see if you are "in the know." *Do you speak the same language.? Can you understand the industry or function vernacular?* In reality, knowing or using these phrases do not reveal your acumen or understanding. It's ironic that the terms that were intended to help explain, now help confuse, exclude, and diminish the value of our ideas and knowledge.

3. **Hot Trend-based Terms.** Similar to clichés, these words are created to explain or categorize the new and unknown. Often thought leaders create these words and concepts as a means to introduce an innovation, be that a new industry, action, or concept. Some of these words fade in and out of popularity depending on their relevance. Often these concepts are used across industries and functions. Their meaning gets pulled and

pinched like taffy, until the point where what once had clear meaning, no longer holds true.

Buzzwords aren't bad necessarily. As you see with the above three types, they began with the intention to explain and unify, but the overuse and misuse have the opposite effect.

Here is how buzzwords turn bad. It's all our fault. We abuse them. We force these hot buzzwords to be broad sweeping, all-encompassing terms that end up losing all meaning to everyone and anyone because we no longer truly understand their meaning. It reminds me of that old Smurf episode, the one where Brainy Smurf explains the Smurf language: *"The Smurf language is basically a variation of a human language where the word 'smurf' is substituted for whatever noun, verb, adjective or adverb being used."*[32] Stop **Smurfizing,** you are ruining perfectly good words.

Buzzwords create **misunderstanding and confusion**. One of the biggest points of failure in any situation is communication. When words become buzz-worthy, their meaning is no longer clear because of so much abuse. Take innovation for example. It's a long-standing term and probably should be inducted into the buzzword hall of fame. The term innovation has become the lipstick of every corporate pig. If you describe a project, product, or idea as innovative, then the assumption is it instantly has cache, regardless if there is anything innovative about it. Unfortunately, its overuse renders the term ineffective in explaining and unifying. It's usually another piece of chart junk on presentations to earn some cache instead of a source of clarity.

Buzzwords **exclude, intimidate, and dismiss**. Let's agree that people use buzzwords with good intentions. But as my mama used to say, "the road to hell is paved with good intentions." Using buzzwords, especially without clarifying, often alienates your audience. People don't want to look or feel dumb, so instead of asking for clarification, that whale of a prospect just walked away without you realizing it. That can add up to reflect significant losses in deals, customers, and partners.

Buzzwords, when misused and misunderstood, **destroy credibility**. If buzzwords are used correctly, they fast track understanding and relevance. But

---

[32] *http://tinyurl.com/smurflanguage*

if you use them to win undue credibility, people recognize it and label you a fraud. Trust can only be acquired through authenticity and transparency. Trust is the cornerstone to innovation and results, so before you think of throwing in a buzzword to beef up your presentation, ensure it is relevant; otherwise, you may just watch your credibility wash down the drain.

Corporate buzzword contortion is one cause of waste in the enterprise, but let's explore how the misunderstanding of a term like *collaboration* can tie up time, mental prowess, and money infinitely. It has become one of the most misused and ill-defined concepts and leads to the **spins** — an endless feedback loop of indecision and inaction. At its core, the word means to work together for a common, productive outcome. I believe in collaboration, as do most people, regardless of title.

In fact, many researchers are calling out "collaboration overload" with the introduction of instant message, email, text, apps, video conferencing software, and a globally dispersed workforce. University professors have studied this phenomenon and warn that it results in stagnation, professional burnout, and employee turnover. Here's what they had to say in a recent article in Harvard Business Review: "We find that what starts as a virtuous cycle soon turns vicious. Soon helpful employees become institutional bottlenecks: Work doesn't progress until they've weighed in. Worse, they are so overtaxed that they're no longer personally effective. And more often than not, the volume and diversity of work they do to benefit others goes unnoticed, because the requests are coming from other units, varied offices, or even multiple companies."[33]

---

[33] *https://hbr.org/2016/01/collaborative-overload*

The research confirms what I've been saying for years. True collaboration cannot be accomplished without deliberation, decision-making, and discipline. And when people misuse the term and take missteps based on that inaccurate understanding, waste is piled on. This is just one example of how a 13-letter word can cost so much. These buzzwords distract and come at a hidden cost that unknowingly drains the enterprise.

One last example of how bad buzzword usage wastes resources is the ability to hide behind them or the confusion they create. In this whirlwind world of today, it's hard to keep up with what everyone is doing and when. It's not like the manufacturing line work of the past where employees clocked in, their output measured by the widgets they produced. The knowledge worker does most of his/her work in their head, so monitoring and measuring can be a challenge. Buzzwords allow some employees to hide, repositioning past work to meet current buzz like some sort of Jedi-mind trick on an overtaxed manager. Others are paralyzed by confusion from these misused words, halting any progress until more clarification is given. Whether intentional gaming or unintentional confusion, these buzzwords are powerful and hurt productivity that could be diverted to innovative efforts that drive results.

Buzzwords **kill buy in, alignment and forward progress**. It is only when buzzwords go bad that they have a negative effect on productivity, innovation, and results. It's such a tempting prospect to use buzzwords to accelerate adoption and understanding, but that is a shallow strategy. Buy-in and alignment must be earned, not bought with a buzzword. As a Leadovator, you must use buzzwords judiciously to set the example. Don't be lured by these siren songs of false relevance and mutual understanding without clarity.

Always remember — big ideas need simple words to be understood, accepted, and shared more broadly. It is your responsibility to assure a transparent, open environment in order to make innovation systemic in the enterprise and lead *The Innovation Revolution*.

**Three Top Tips, to help you take the buzz out of buzzwords and vigilantly communicate clearly to increase productivity, innovation and results:**

1. **Check yourself before you wreck yourself.** If you read any of those emotional intelligence books or take classes, you will surely get this one. You must be keenly self-aware. You must clearly understand who you are trying to communicate with and what you are trying to communicate.

If you have doubts your audience may misinterpret, listen to your gut. Change your words or your graphics to be more clear.

**Simplify** is your action verb. It is your mantra. The less jargon and the less buzzwords, the easier for people to understand. I often run my presentations and communications by peers who are not in my industry. They do the same. We are a two-way sounding board. Sure, it takes a little more time upfront, but the comprehension and the activation more than make up for the pre-game time investment.

2. **You know what happens when you ass-u-me.** Assumptions get us in trouble. Even if you know your audience or your team like your own family, it is best to not assume. I always pretend I am talking to my 80-year-old grandma when I prepare to speak to a group or within my team. My grandma just learned how to text, so you can imagine how much simplification that forces on me. While I never dumb-down things, I do ensure I have communicated what I mean by a certain buzzword or popular concept and define my interpretation of the subject to absolutely ensure everyone is on my page. This action offers you an ability to personalize your message. You add your spin or experience to it vs. letting the blogosphere, pundits, or other talking heads dominate and own certain words and phrases.

3. **Dear Prudence … use these beat up buzzwords with great caution.** There is always a time and place for things and using buzzwords is no different. As I explained previously, buzzwords never meant to be so bad, their very creation was intended to explain and unify. It is only the overuse

> "Authenticity is a powerful force. Don't ruin it with an illusion."

or *smurfizing* of these terms that dilute their meaning and value. You must be prudent when using these terms. You must ensure they are relevant to your outcome. You must judge if they will help your big ideas spread faster and reach a broader audience instead of alienating or dismissing members of your audience. I always say, "never use a 50-cent word when a penny one will do." You don't need big-headed buzzwords to amplify your idea. You must have the confidence and courage to share it as it is. Because in this highly distracted world we live and work in, complexity will miss the mark and you may not have another chance.

This should get you started. Authenticity is a powerful force, don't ruin it with an illusion.

# THE Weekly ZING

## Your Innovation Challenge
## The Swear Jar

Remember the old swear jars, you know when you had to pay if you said a bad word?

What common business terms would you like to fine? Maybe leverage, synergy, collaboration, cross-functional… Now you think of a few more and try to avoid them. Come up with an alternative and see if it catches on.

**One Up It:** Bring your version of the swear jar to your next meeting, and a list of those banned words.
Call out a team member for using one of these tired words and charge him/her a dollar. You can always give the money to charity or treat them all to a vending machine treat.

Share your banned words with @48Innovate use #swearjar #businesbingo.

# Chapter 8

# Introducing Smart Speed: A Mindset, a Method, and a Movement

*"I never lose. I either win or learn."*

*— Nelson Mandela*

Promise of Chapter:

- Introduce your antidote to business-as-usual and path to systemic innovation.
- Detail the tangible and intangible components of this mindset and method.
- Prepare you for a mind shift to strategic agility through self-awareness.

*What is Smart Speed?*

- It's a mindset, a method, and a movement away from the madness.
- It's facilitated a billion in new revenue for Fortune 50 companies in a fraction of the time and money of traditional methods.
- It's the Leadovator's best chance to evolving the internal risk-averse dysfunction that halts innovation into an effective systemic innovation engine to lead *The Innovation Revolution*.

  *"Most people are afraid of what will happen when they go outside the lines."*

- It's a transformation vehicle, a movement to save the enterprise among all the disruptive chaos. Most people are afraid of what will happen when they go outside the lines. This method successfully takes them outside and instills trust and confidence in a new way of doing things through successful execution.

- It's a bridge to the new normal, allowing employees up and down the stack to learn how to successfully introduce and execute innovation as a habit and matter of course, not as an anomaly.
- It gives everyone permission to relearn, to be pre-educated, to be beginners again, without shame or insecurity.
- It removes the toxic political environment through transparency, process, and fairness. It engages, develops, and delivers.

## Smart Speed Provides:

*Speed to ideas.*
*Speed to decisions.*
*Speed to results.*
*Speed with empathy.*
*Speed with employee engagement.*
*Speed with intelligence and confidence.*

It's the only way to unlearn bad business habits, embrace change as a superpower, and capitalize on the chaos for competitive advantage.

## A Smart Speed Success

Everyone needs proof and here is mine. This is one of many case studies from my company 48 Innovate, which facilitates the Smart Speed Method for medium and large companies to deliver systemic innovation.

The challenge for Cisco™ Commercial South Sales leadership was clear. Annual sales planning with a geographically scattered and busy leadership team took almost six weeks of scheduled and rescheduled meetings — too long to be efficient and meet market demand.

Also, the process involved leadership only, leaving team members removed from decision-making. Studies show that this decision-making gap is a prime reason large technology companies like Cisco lose talent to innovate startups.

Enter 48 Innovate, a two-day experience that infuses a nimble entrepreneurial spirit into the world of big business, and changes organizations from the ground up.

## The Smart Speed Method at Work:

- Thirty-five people from across all functions of Cisco Commercial South Sales were invited to a boutique hotel in the eclectic mountain city of Asheville, NC.

- The participants were armed with information. Our 48 Innovate Team worked in advance with Cisco leadership to set measurable goals and disseminate real market data to participants, similar to the kick off activities of most strategy management consultant engagements, except without the suits and the million-dollar price tag.

- Invitees were challenged to each come prepared with a 60-second pitch to grow business by 20%.

In return, Cisco Commercial South leadership committed to adopting the winning presentation as a part of their sales strategy, without knowing the outcome. Brave. Group executives were just as involved in the process as individual participants, serving as coaches and final judges. As a result, the level of participation and buy-in was high across the board.

48 Innovate over-delivered, generating not one, but two viable plans with specific and actionable business cases for 20% growth. Cisco Commercial South leadership implemented both within a year and beat market expectations.

One 48 Innovate participant said this about the experience, "No celebrity appearances or laser light shows; just smart people skipping the usual corporate dance, rolling up their sleeves, and sharing their best ideas." What a perfect description of Smart Speed.

48 Innovate took away high marks from Cisco participants. Exit surveys generated an average rating of 4.93 out of a possible 5, with attendees describing their experiences as ... *awesome ... well planned and executed without being micro-managed — bravo!*

Time saver, team builder, leadership tool, idea incubator, and actionable plan creator—Cisco Commercial South executives called 48 Innovate one of the best investments their group has ever made! All participants mastered Smart Speed without even knowing it — decisive, collaborative, and fast.

Annette Blum, Director of Business Strategy for Cisco Commercial South Sales, exclaimed, "What a great tool for team engagement and buy-in ... plus, we streamlined a process that normally takes six weeks of meetings into just two short days!"

Given the right mindset, inputs, and process, Smart Speed delivers today and beyond.

The need for speed has always existed in business and throughout history. The only thing that has changed is scale and pace. The pace has accelerated. We have already explored many modern driving forces of the new, hyper-drive business normal in part one of this book. The necessity of faster innovation and faster releases continues to drive behavior of organizations and the people within them. However, pure speed is nothing without function, intelligence, and value. Remember the Aesop fable, *The Tortoise and the Hare*, taught us the lesson that pure speed and over-confidence doesn't always win the race. Think of Smart Speed as a hybrid, a "TortoHare." Consistent, thoughtful actions, be that products, processes, or just everyday decisions, taken confidently and with good intentions at an accelerated rate that delivers.

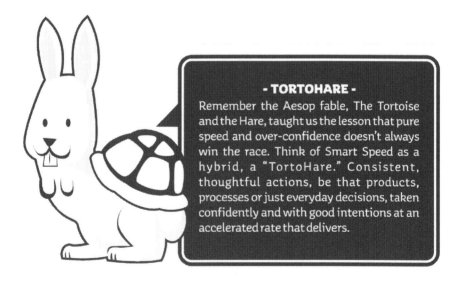

**- TORTOHARE -**

Remember the Aesop fable, The Tortoise and the Hare, taught us the lesson that pure speed and over-confidence doesn't always win the race. Think of Smart Speed as a hybrid, a "TortoHare." Consistent, thoughtful actions, be that products, processes or just everyday decisions, taken confidently and with good intentions at an accelerated rate that delivers.

This Smart Speed Method includes both the tangible and intangible elements to follow in order to usher the desired results. Let's start with the intangible — the magic, the mindset, the perspective, and the attitude. The process and tools are the easy part. The mindset shift offers the greatest challenge in this evolutionary process.

Smart Speed requires the nimble entrepreneurial spirit combined with the poised scaling approach of the enterprise. Startups and entrepreneurs successfully command agility, acting on imperfect information at a moment's notice, pivoting or changing course in a blink, iteratively testing features and processes with their customers to remain infinitely relevant as the market and needs shift. Conversely, enterprise leaders dominate scale and measured response, delivering products and services to the globe through vast infrastructure, steady cash flow, and experience. The combination is the key to leverage Smart Speed to transform your entire organization into a sustainable innovation engine. It's evolving at the cell level of the organization.

The ideal mindset to leading *The Innovation Revolution* is one of strategic agility.

- It's the ability to confidently embrace a constant state of ambiguity and yet decisively lead a team, an organization, or a market forward.
- It's knowing that your decisions are more directions instead of destinations.
- It's juggling trials, errors, and expansion at the same time.
- It's activating empathy within a complex interconnected matrix of stakeholder interests inside and out.
- It's balancing short-, mid-, and long-term results..
- It's reframing failures as research, learning and more information for the next decision in the continuum.
- It's welcoming the challenge of a condensed strategic horizon of 18-36 months instead of the recent benchmark of 3-5 years.
- It's letting go of the white-knuckle grip of the past, the permanent and the perfect.

Simple, right? Ok, don't freak out just yet. **Breathe.** There is a solution.

There are only two beliefs enterprise leaders must change to lead *The Innovation Revolution* and operationalize innovation:

1.  The incessant need for perfection, and
2.  The fear of the fallout without it.

These two beliefs are the fundamental reasons why medium to large companies can't pivot on a dime. Don't get me wrong; they have enormously expedited their processes from the past. And, the market, with all those nipping startups and empowered consumers, has forced their hand, but the enterprise pace is still behind. Indecision and inaction are the result of those debilitating beliefs and is what slows everything to a sloth's pace.

Let me validate that epic fear of failure and the imperfect. In school, no one explicitly tells you how powerful zeros can be. When you are talking about millions and billions and a global audience, there is a lot more to lose for an enterprise company than a startup that has less than 100 employees, a couple of years in the market, and a small board of investors to appease.

Two perfect examples of legendary enterprise failures that people are still talking about: New Coke™ and Crystal Pepsi™. The global beverage titans both had misfires with new product introductions. More important than the failures in those cases is the fact that both companies rallied and thrived despite them. You see, that's what we have to remember. Perfection doesn't exist, and if you don't take the risk to innovate or move beyond the safety of your current cash cow, your future is definitely in peril. Anybody remember Blockbuster™? Enough said.

Let me further complicate this mindset transformation with an admission — management strategy and methodology over the last 30 years has intentionally slowed the pace of action and decision. It is a big, fat safety valve and a means of control. From big movements like Total Quality Management Control to Six Sigma to regulatory accounting and policies like Sarbanes-Oxley, organizations have purposely put in systems and processes to prevent hasty or reckless decisions and outcomes. When an organization reaches a certain size, process, systems, and approval chains are the only logical way to manage. It makes sense that no one person in a 10,000+ company can know or make decisions on everything at the same time for everyone. It's impossible.

- STRATEGIC AGILITY -

Grounding in that past, it is for you to view this Smart Speed Method as a means to evolve — the next phase in leadership and management.

In review of the first, most important and difficult part of the method, Smart Speed requires a mindset shift to strategic agility for everyone up, down, and around the organizational chain. Leaders must set the example for not only employees, but also partners, customers, and stakeholders. It cannot be lip service or empty buzzword bingo. It must be demonstrated through actions, decisions, engagement, and empowerment.

Don't worry, we will get to the "how" in detail, but for now, let's explore the next component of the Smart Speed Method: the inputs or the resources. We could write a whole book about resources — how to get them, how to allocate them, how to optimize them, how to reallocate them, but that is not the focus. We will briefly touch on three major inputs or resources: time, money, and people and how they factor into this new method.

The thing about time is this: you can't make any more of it, and, sometimes you lose it without warning. Time is a nonrenewable resource. I'm not going to go all Stephen Hawking on you, but time keeps ticking regardless of how we treat it. Fundamentally, the Smart Speed Method requires us to manage time differently and with the respect it deserves. We aspire to use it wisely, but so often we abuse it. The previous chapters demonstrated how we waste it — in meetings, on email, or spinning in indecision. That is just plain time abuse. Smart Speed requires that we face all the waste and make a different choice. It is a choice to become time transformers by reallocating and optimizing.[34]

The Smart Speed Method creates a sense of urgency and compels us to focus. It forces us to finally admit multitasking destroys progress by some false sense of alignment and inclusion. Smart Speed compels us to pause

---

[34] http://www.economist.com/news/briefing/21679448-pace-business-really-getting-quicker-creed-speed

- IMPACT VELOCITY -

before we race and then race before we perish. It's a delicate balance, and we are all terrible at balance. We so passionately want to do more of what's working, which usually ends in a destructive over-rotation. But that balance offers a killer prize — impact velocity.

**Time** in Smart Speed is used to first, freeze all the distractions and infinite variables and scenarios to absorb the intelligence, data and goals, and pin-point a singular, objective focal point. Just as it is impossible for one person to manage everything at every moment for everyone, it is impossible for leaders, teams, or organizations to capitalize on every opportunity, large and small. Niche markets, micro messaging, and poignant laser-light targeting is the only way to break through all the noise and clutter of today. The freeze is an opportunity to stop all the *what ifs*, collect the information available at that moment, and decide on an objective, measureable goal. Note: I didn't say destination or decision or product or services or any other finite, prescriptive path. Just an objective, a goal, such as growth by X%. That is a direction, not a destination. That is an opportunity to guide all other resources to the optimal path.

After the freeze-frame, time in Smart Speed is used next to focus, inspire, and align. After the objective measurable goal is set, the next interval is to pose this challenge to a diverse group of knowledgeable and ideally cross-functional employees (possibly partners and customers too, if you are so brave), to take that challenge and with intelligence, data, and institutional wisdom to create possible solutions to deliver that specific goal.

Then, literally, the method requires time for those interest-aligned employees to focus on this challenge and nothing else — not their day job, not all the fires that start or burn ongoing in the organization, but a focused time just to pitch, filter, create, and present a compelling solution backed by experience, data, and validation. In the field-tested trials we performed through 48 Innovate, 48 hours or two days is the optimal timeframe for this activity. A half-day or day is too short and doesn't allow for some overnight brain processing, and three days or beyond offers too much time for indecision and innovation fatigue. That focus and sense of urgency deliver the best possible solutions without second-guessing, and force alignment and buy-in through the collaborative process. Time is a powerful tool in the Smart Speed Method.

And, as a side note, *timing* is different than time itself. Timing has a lot to do with luck. And since we can't formally manage luck, let's not get distracted by that notion.

**Money.** The answer to everything and nothing at the same time. Too often we use money as the excuse or response to every issue. No one can argue the power of money to drive impact, when used appropriately and wisely. In large organizations, money is misallocated, and in small ones, it's just not available to allocate at all. These are fundamentally two opposing issues to two extremely different entities. But Smart Speed necessitates the allocation or reallocation of funds toward a common, aligned solution to the objective, measurable goal. Investing in the right solution vs. the known solution (an example of **legacy inertia**) is the biggest hurdle for this resource challenge and the Smart Speed Method offers collective wisdom, buy-in, and a validating process to confidently invest with the information available at decision time. Today's asynchronous, yet linear, internal processes don't efficiently or effectively produce these key ingredients for change.

**People.** The messy, gnarly, can't-live-with-and-can't-live-without resource we must properly manage to make any strides forward. This unpredictable, necessary resource puzzles everyone. People are the rule and the exception to the rule. Their dynamic and fickle behavior is exactly why everything's so temporary, uncertain, and ambiguous. Smart Speed requires an allowance for the unknown to accommodate the X factor in people, while acknowledging their wisdom, necessity, and impact. The process is guided to allow enough confidence and trust to enable innovation and change without the halting effect of fear.

The word choice of "people" was purposeful. It includes employees of all types and titles. It includes customers and prospects. It includes partners too. People, human beings, are at the center of the method. Recognizing their necessity and more importantly, their unexpected brilliance, is the key to Smart Speed and delivering systemic innovation in the enterprise. INTRApreneurs, entrepreneurs, maintainers, experienced and inexperience, regardless of affinity or status, Smart Speed leverages them all to fulfill the organization's destiny. It requires vulnerability. It requires faith in a time of infinite data. It requires space in a crowded forum. It requires courage from leaders and participants combined to deliver.

Finally, we will explore the application of Smart Speed — the scalable, repeatable process to maximize innovation, action, and results, systemically and sustainably within the enterprise. Remember there are no quick fixes in this *Innovation Revolution*. Attitude, behavior, and culture must evolve through practice over time.

Here is the simple Smart Speed Process.™

Preparation
Pitch
Vote
Teamup
Create
Present
Follow up

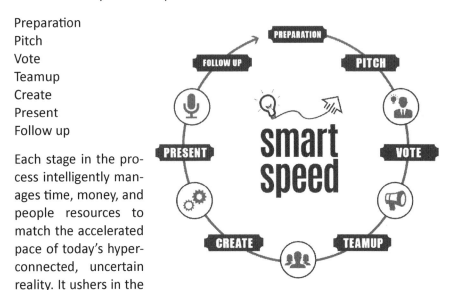

Each stage in the process intelligently manages time, money, and people resources to match the accelerated pace of today's hyper-connected, uncertain reality. It ushers in the transformation to operationalized innovation.

The Smart Speed methodology incorporates standard business management practices you learned in b-school or on the job, combined with lean startup methodologies. It provides the velocity needed to capture market transitions and dynamic customer needs with the poise, control, and constraints of large global scale and dissemination. It integrates empathy across a matrix of organization stakeholders inside and out. And, it works! More than $1 billion in revenue-generating, employee executed projects delivered in less than two years from Fortune 500 companies to mid-size INC 500 and beyond, at a fraction of the cost and time of traditional methods.

In the era of accelerated pace of change, unprecedented user experience, a revolution of startups and entrepreneurship, and changing workforce dynamics, the process seamlessly weaves principles in strategic planning, ideation, design thinking, lean startup methodology, modern learning, and development science, active employee engagement methods and change management and leadership in a fun, high energy, accelerated experience that creates measureable impact to organizations at Smart Speed.

The proven Smart Speed methodology drives innovation, simplicity, and customer focus that typically produces employee-created 20-40 flash innovation ideas and five to seven business case solutions to a pre-defined measureable challenge. This process is guided by a certified Solutionator, or Smart Speed Facilitator, trained to balance fear and reality through a managed process to create an uncertain, yet targeted measurable outcome. It facilitates the strategic agility mindset from start to finish. It is a Leadovator's solution to transition the enterprise into this new normal and deliver systemic innovation throughout the organization, instead of just piecemeal pockets, and lead the charge in *The Innovation Revolution*.

There are 7 stages to usher Smart Speed successfully today and in the future. You will see them in the next chapter.

That's it in a nutshell. The strategic agility mindset, properly engaged resources applied to a simple, yet powerful process that skips the slow corporate dance or business-as-usual to drive innovation and impact at Smart Speed, continuously.

*Wondering what to do next?* First, don't believe the PR in your head or your organization that you are already doing this, because that is not true. Sure, there may be pockets of this type of activity here and there, but it is not consistent, nor systematic, and it is very limited.

*Remember way back in part one of this book, where you did all this assessing?* Now it's time to reflect back on those assessments about yourself, your organization, and your employees. Think about these concepts relative to those assessment outcomes. Self-awareness is the first step in transformation.

**Step 1. Be honest with yourself and ask if you believe the two barrier beliefs to Smart Speed: the need for perfection and the fear of not having it.**

Maybe you don't know, but your actions will reveal the truth. *Do you do any of the following? Do your peers or executive leadership?* These are indicating actions that the beliefs are present.

    a. Do you push off decisions more than once to gather more data?

    b. Do you spend hours and evenings on tweaking an executive presentation?

    c. Do you lobby to hire an old-guard consulting firm on projects more than 2 years in a row?

   d. Do you always change your employees project overviews or presentations?

   e. Do you spin failures with a complex story with multiple groups and people involved?

   f. Is your motive behind getting other leaders names on a project for buy-in or for a fail-safe?

It's hard to say whether you answer yes or no to these questions, if you believe those impeding ideas, because most of the time you are unaware of your real motives for making certain decisions. We hide from ourselves when fear is the motivator, because it makes us feel weak. Vulnerability hasn't been celebrated in the past. Know that even your own assessment may be biased. Just notice in the coming weeks as you make decisions or take actions. *Do you see the pattern above?* Examine what motivates those choices and see if insights emerge.

**Step 2. Whatever your role in the organization, it's important to take stock in the usage of the three top resources: Time, Money and People.**

   a. Are employees wasting time on busywork?

   b. Is throwing money at a problem the first thought or suggestion?

   c. Are the people in the wrong place? Are you leveraging the ecosystem - inside, outside or around -- of people resources effectively?

**Step 3. Take an inventory of all the innovation initiatives in your organization.**

You will be surprised how many disparate projects and processes are at play.

- *Are these activities consistent?*
- *Is there follow through and accountability?*
- *Are they in service of real overarching impact to the business?*
- *Are they contributing to speed of decision-making and action?*
- *Are employees, partners, and customers involved in the creation and execution?*

Only by knowing the current state of your organization will you better apply these principles and usher transformation. In the famous words of Pema Chodron, "Clarity and decisiveness come from the willingness to slow down, to listen to and look at what is happening."

## THE Weekly ZING

# Your Innovation Challenge
# Pivot Power

Think of an obstacle in your current project. Try the old pivot and turn.

Turn away from your current obstacle.

Look for a new opening, what are ways around this obstacle – over, under, through, around.

Write down these solutions and bring them up to your team in your next project status meeting. The important thing is to keep moving toward the goal.

Share your insights with @48Innovate use #PivotPower.

# Chapter 9

# Smart Speed: The Details

*"It's all in the practice."*

*— Lauryn Hill*

Promise of the Chapter:

- Explain the details and mechanics of the Smart Speed process.
- Reveal how this method is a tool to allow others to experience success outside the lines.
- Offer three actions to ignite this employee-driven process and begin the transition.

We all know as common sense that smart, quick decisions and execution deliver results. In 2012, Bain & Company researchers surveyed executives worldwide from 760 companies with revenues exceeding $1 billion, to understand whether decisions were made faster or slower than competitors among other decision effectiveness. They found decision effectiveness and financial results correlated at a 95% confidence level or higher for every country, industry, and company size. This data confirms that effective decisions equal better financial results — we already knew that, right?

Most respondents rated the speed of decision-making much lower or on par with its competitors and more than 80% of respondents said that decisions required too much effort.

Yet another confirmation that the best way to get ahead of competitors, is to reduce the time and effort it takes to make a decision in an organization.[35] The Smart Speed Method does that and so much more. It teaches

---

[35] *http://www.bain.com/publications/articles/measuring-decision-effectiveness.aspx*

employee participants how to make data-driven, confident decisions and empowers them to take action on those decisions to provide value as a habit, not as a one off. If you are going to operationalize innovation, you can't keep control in the hands of the few. You must transfer confidence and responsibility deeper within the organization. And in order to be comfortable with letting that control go, you must teach others how through practice.

## Another Smart Speed Success

Smart Speed isn't just for giants like Cisco; medium high-growth companies realize extreme benefits too. All organizations face similar issues of traction and adoption when ushering in change and innovation. Focus and buy-in play crucial roles in the process.

In a word — GROWTH! Fourteen-year-old security technology startup Lancope™ wanted to make the most of its success (and venture funding) with a plan that would fuel 50% growth per year over the next five years.

The top 25 global network security firm had also doubled its workforce in just a few months, creating a need to blend "old" and "new" employees into a cohesive unit with shared goals and vision.

Bridge the divisions by bringing together 32 Lancope employees from multiple departments for a major injection of start-up culture (i.e. innovate and think outside the job description) to offer customer benefits, solve problems, and drive achievement of goals company-wide.

Old meets new. Engineers partner with customer service representatives. Financial folks engage with marketing teams. Sales interacts with operational leads. Executives serve as team coaches and judges.

Everyone is engaged, invested, a stakeholder. And there's a stopwatch to corral the innovation and keep it all on time. (*How many internal planning or brainstorming sessions can you say that about?*)

Using this unique format and Lancope's number one resource, its people, 48 Innovate helped teams generate not one, but three actionable plans that the company is in various stages of implementing — a fast track for a SaaS™ offering, a renewal loyalty program, and a consumer-like incentive model to save time while building more intelligence into its products.

That's a win, win, win!

Lancope Chief Technology Officer TK Keanini says, "It creates constraints that truly foster innovation and delivers."

Lancope successfully infused its maturing company with start-up brand energy and practices, reinvigorating the culture that made it great. It mastered Smart Speed and positioned itself for future success.

On the human side, bonds were formed across all levels of employees. The workforce was empowered and engaged. New and old employees were equally passionate and invested.

One participant sums it up well. "It brought together so many different parts of the company and gave us a platform to work with others with whom we wouldn't otherwise engage. Plus, the sense that your project could have a significant impact on the company as a whole is extremely exciting."

Finally, management is now backing three exciting new plans for significant growth created in just 48 hours. CFO and COO David Cocchiara said, "The buy-in on all levels, the infusion of a collective passion, and the assimilation of our vision throughout the team, enabled the company to produce real actionable results from this experience." And yes, he vows to use the Smart Speed process again.

The 7-stage process beginning with up-front preparation followed by in-session facilitation through follow up and execution, delivers for companies of all sizes, in all stages.

Smart Speed delivers REAL WORLD, REAL RESULTS in just 48 hours.

Your basic overview of Smart Speed as a concept has whet your appetite. Let's pull back the curtain and show you the wizard and the science behind the magic. The most important element in this process are your employees — those natural or soon-to-be INTRApreneurs, trained and empowered to deliver. The process is based on igniting employee-driven innovation consistently and at Smart Speed. It's based on cultivating INTRApreneurs instead of minions. It's a transformational approach that will challenge the status quo through successful experiences doing things differently. When executed again and again, the process stops the automatic "NO" to new ideas, and it allows your workforce up and down the hierarchy to build strength and confidence in a new way of doing things. With repeated success, a new approach will become the new normal — the NEW business-as-usual that delivers systemic innovation.

## The Details — How the Method Works and Why

Let's explore the **7-Stage Smart Speed Methodology**™ that facilitates systemic results-bearing innovation in greater detail. This method is based on your employees being the generators, presenters, and executors, leveraging the talent you already have and institutional knowledge to facilitate co-creation and accelerate decision-making through execution. It positions employees as the consultants, mindful of their impact to the business on a visceral level. They no longer feel detached from the organization's success, but embrace their true role as shared owners. It literally transforms them into inside entrepreneurs, a.k.a. INTRApreneurs.

This is an event-based process, which allows for focus and momentum, but also causes limited disruption in critical daily business operations. This eliminates the usual waste and productivity killers and stops multitasking in its tracks. The event-based process is a microcosm of all the elements needed to overcome business-as-usual, but in time and with practice all these elements and behaviors will become natural and interwoven in the operations of the organization and goes far beyond the enabling event process. The method includes a preliminary planning and preparation stage, followed by a 48-hour innovation event, and a series of follow ups to ensure accountability and execution. A certified Smart Speed Solutionator is essential to this method. (Don't worry. It doesn't have to be an outsider, you can train an insider to stoke the fire to continuously facilitate for sustained momentum). Here are the typical timeframes for each stage:

- Planning & Preparation: 5-6 weeks.
- Unite, Pitch, Teamup, Create, Present and Judge: 48 hours.
- Follow up: 90 days, with a progress check-in every 30 days to ensure a project plan for implementation.
- Execution: 3–18 months depending on project scope.
- Post-Execution Check in: 12-18 months, depending on the project scope.

If your inner cynic is bubbling up, let me address that before we move forward. *If you are asking, how is this event-based model the path to operationalizing innovation? Isn't it another spot activity?* If you do it just once, absolutely. This is a tool for your organization's evolution. It must be executed repeatedly to build confidence, fast track innovation execution, and undo all the dysfunctional internal processes, systems, and cultural norms of today, with less resistance and pain. The process is rewiring culture from within. It is allowing all your employees to eventually have a successful shared experience in a new way of doing things, while producing results. It is negating the command and control of the past and replacing it with effective disciplined collaboration that produces better solutions at speed.

Now that we have silenced that cynic, let's explore the stages and necessary actions to execute this method within your organization.

## 7-Stage Smart Speed Methodology

### STAGE 1: Planning and Preparation

*No brainer, right?* You must first prepare and plan before embarking on any project, especially for an innovation one. Included in this stage are some critical components to ensure all the elements are in place to move at Smart Speed.

First you must understand your specific measurable objective or the famous 1980s concept for setting objectives, S.M.A.R.T. (Specific, Measurable, Attainable, Realistic, Time-related), originally presented by consultant George T. Doran in his paper, *There's a S.M.A.R.T Way to write management Goals and Objectives.*[36] Discipline is critical for this step. So often in the haste or overwhelmed schedules of leaders, we wing it on this one. It is common that leaders establish a series of "and" goals, which dilute focus and cause confusion. For example, we need to grow by 15% and we need to reduce costs by 15% and we need to *<insert a series of other measureable goals that complicate the objective>*. There are always a complex series of goals a company wants to strive to meet, but it is important when focusing on innovation that you simplify and create an overarching objective that is specific enough, but offers some room for different ideas and approaches.

---

[36] *Doran, George T. There's a S.M.A.R.T Way to write management Goals and Objectives. Spokane, WA. November 1981.*

This measurable objective is woven into the preparation materials for participants and the judging criteria for the innovation event itself and for the post-event follow up to align start to finish. Clarity is a powerful force.

### Action 1. Preparation Stage: Establish an Overarching S.M.A.R.T. Goal.

It includes a measureable goal within a certain timeframe to set the scope. We have found 12 months is best, since organizations always work within a fiscal year, but no more than 18 months, because of the pace of change in the marketplace. Here is an example of a S.M.A.R.T. challenge goal: Create a ready-to-implement plan to grow the business by 20% within the next 12 months.

Leaders are forced to focus on a theme or topic and present a clearly stated goal, in which we can measure effectiveness in the judging criteria of the event, as well as the follow up and execution of the winning plan.

The next part of the preparation and planning phase of this framework is divided into three actions:

- Selecting participants.
- Gathering data and information.
- Planning the 48-hour innovation event.

### Action 2. Preparation Stage: Selecting Participants for Your Innovation Event.

The event is a key component of the model. It allows for your employees and stakeholders to focus on the task at hand. As we have already discussed, multitasking is not only killing productivity, it is affecting the quality of your output. This allows teams to take a limited time out of the day-to-day to innovate. It also takes them out of their routine. This disruption offers a different perspective. You can't envision anything different if you are surrounded by the same things all the time.

The unique part of this event is in the preparation, set up, participant roles and the follow up.

**There are three participant roles for this event:**

1. **Employee Participants**. These are your top cross-functional employees that have those INTRApreneurial qualities we reviewed in Part One and who will create the solutions to the challenge question. Typically, in a 48

Innovate event, there are 20-50 employee participants. These participants will be required to pitch a 60-second idea to solve that measureable challenge question on event day.

There are two ways to select these employee participants, while keeping in mind that diversity is a key ingredient both in skill, mindset and role. Multiple perspectives produce more viable solutions:

a. Offer an application process or volunteer option to participate - you may need to stack the deck by encouraging a diverse set of high potentials to apply

b. Offer a reward for high potentials and excellent performers

2. **Coaches or Advisors.** These are your subject matter experts (SMEs). These participants steer the event teams and guide them to a solution that is viable and validated. These participants may be business unit leaders, internal SMEs, external partners, or customers. They can be in person or virtual.

3. **Judges.** These are your executives who are willing to make a decision on an initiative and can move resources — budget and/or people — to execute the solution.

The advisors and judges are selected based on their expertise, influence, and relevance to the challenge. Often they are usually the sponsoring organization and the cross-functional stakeholders.

A best practice gained from these events is to include a customer or partner participant. It allows for easy access to validate assumptions and to co-create with your stakeholders. It's scary to reveal the messy process with your external stakeholders, but it is the only way to validate your solution. It will allow you to work out the kinks way before scaling.

Selecting these roles is critical to success. You must ensure that all participants have relevant knowledge to solve the focused challenge. You must also ensure you have the key advisors and influencers to help fast track these solutions. Innovation fails because of lack of adoption. The best way to mitigate that risk is to build buy-in during the creation process. This type of event allows for relationship-building, validation, and buy-in built in across the matrix of stakeholders. In addition, this event creates innovation champions to help influence the greater organization at roll out.

**Action 3. Preparation Stage: Gathering Data and Information to Support the S.M.A.R.T. Challenge.**

Just like when you engage with any external help, you must gather background information for them. You will do the same exercise for your employee-driven innovation event. It should include:

- Historical data: Think financials, sales, marketing, or operational data.
- Trend data of the industry, geography or function such as Gartner, Forrester, or government reports.
- Anecdotal or testimonial information from customers, partners, or employees.

This data gathering and dissemination is all in service for everyone to be literally on the same page. Often teams aren't working from the same data set and that causes confusion and tension, which impedes decision and action.

Don't over think it. There is an infinite amount of information and not an infinite amount of time to review, filter, and apply. Put together a data packet that would be enough for you or your leadership team to make an assessment and decision, and you will be set. Plus, participants will bring their own knowledge and research to the table as well.

Something to always keep in mind is the fact there is never really a lack of data; there is only a lack of analysis and application of that data.

Don't worry about getting this data pack together weeks in advance. No one will look at it until they need it. We find that a week with a weekend before the big event is plenty of time for people to review and leverage. Plus, throughout the event, participants will continue to reference that data packet as they create their business case presentation for judging.

**Action 4. Preparation Stage: Planning the 48-Hour Innovation Event.**

Next up is event logistics to usher in a successful 48-hour innovation event. Not just any event plan will do. In order to facilitate fast-tracked innovation and decision making, there are some critical steps. This is where a large portion of the Smart Speed methodology is executed: *Pitch, Vote, Teamup, Create, & Present.*

You must set a date. It is critical the event is held on two consecutive days. If you try to break it up, you will dilute the momentum and significantly slow down the process. The sense of urgency is part of the magic and science. Studies have proven that taking more time to make decisions doesn't improve the outcome. It usually only allows more opportunity for doubt. Plus, this format allows for focus and engagement among team members to build relationships, which is an essential side benefit. Relationships are key to productive communities of learning, sharing, and activation, especially if they are managed by a matrix reporting structure, and when they are geographically dispersed. They also seed cultural change, since you are trying to change business-as-usual.

Selecting the right environment and location is the next step. Ideally, you will go off-site where participants can be free from distraction and the business-as-usual thinking. If that isn't an option, no biggie. You need at least one large room where all 50 participants can fit for the kick off and judging close. You will also need breakout spaces for the working teams; usually five to seven teams emerge from the pitch session in the beginning. Set aside five to seven areas for teams to work. They don't have to be separate rooms; just enough space to work.

Next up is the agenda and timeline for the 48 Innovate event. Every moment is planned for this activity to maximize a very small amount of time. Within the 48-hour innovation agenda there are networking and social activities. The team doesn't work 48 hours straight. And every event must close with a celebration or after party. This immersive and intense experience requires all of these elements to build the bonds of trust to enable accelerated decisions and seed all the after-effects of this event among your team and into your organization.

And, yes, you ABSOLUTELY have to have an after party. Think about the amount of work, passion, and soul that these participants have exerted on behalf of the company.

- They have pushed the limits of their comfort zones over and over in order to innovate on behalf of the organization.
- They have overcome the usual "storming and norming" challenges of teamwork.
- They have endured pivot after pivot of their idea to create an actionable plan that brings real-live-no-jive value to the organization.

The energy, passion and bonds built in this small amount of time are solidified with a fun celebration. The after party is non-negotiable.

Finally, you need to prepare and execute event communication. This includes invitations to participants explaining the event, their pre-activation homework, and their role.

Preparation communications should include the following:

- Event logistics and clarification.
- Event goal and measureable challenge objective.
- Data packet and 60-second pitch assignment.
- Tips, tricks and a series of micro-education about pitch tips, lean startup methods, and other innovation best practices to prepare them for this action-packed innovation experience.
- Pre-kick off meeting or call to review the event, homework, and expectations (always a nice-to-have since everyone feels like they are stepping out of their comfort zone).

We find that creating an event landing page showcasing employee participants as the talent and experts they are gives them an excellent confidence boost. The landing page also serves as a one stop shop for all the relevant information to keep the teams engaged throughout the whole process.

### STAGES 2 –7: 48 Innovate Experience — Pitch, Vote, Teamup, Create & Present

These five critical stages are included in the 48-hour innovation event itself. You have prepped, communicated and engaged your selected employee participants for this big innovation experience. The measureable challenge has been set. Your participants have arrived to get down and innovate.

Usually the 48 Innovate event starts with a brief executive open. I mean brief, say 15 minutes or so. Then it is followed by a review of the goal, what to expect, the specific judging criteria for the final presentation, and then an icebreaker to get everyone confident and loose.

### STAGE 2: Pitch

Then, it's on. Each of the employee participants prepared a 60-second pitch to solve the measurable challenge question beforehand.  Pitches must held to the strictest of time standards. We use a big iPad™ or clock so the pitch person sees how much time they have. No one gets any more time than 60 seconds. We cheer everyone on like rock stars to kick off their pitch and then clap them off when time is up. This raises the energy-level in the whole room. It also builds confidence, support and trust among all the participants to facilitate creative and innovative ideas and collaboration.

One important note here is that the pitches on day one are not the actual results for judging. They are just a starting point, a series of themes. They are pre-filtered brainstorming. It fast tracks the usual brainstorming activity by forcing individuals to validate before with the data packet or others and make their best choice. So relax, this is all a part of the process. Giving up control is the hardest part.

Part of this exercise is to help teach employees how to concisely communicate their ideas to their peers and managers. By the way, during this activity there are no slides, no videos, and no computers allowed for the pitches. No EXCEPTIONS. Remember, you are teaching new habits. If you want to stop all the busywork, slide slave and Excel jockeying, you must have everyone, including managers and executives experience a different way of communicating.

This is rapid fire. One after another, the individuals pitch their best idea on how the organization can solve their big challenge within a certain timeframe, i.e., 12–18 months. After an employee participant pitches, they write the name of their idea and a few key bullets about their idea on a giant sticky note and post it in the room.

The room is filled with all innovative ideas from the collective. It is wallpapered with the best and brightest from your teams. And it facilitates the next stage — **Vote.**

## STAGE 3: Vote

This stage uses the power of the crowd to narrow the 20–50 ideas into five to seven viable themes for consideration and creation. Everyone, including the coaches/advisors and the judges, gets the same amount of votes each. Everyone is equal. During this stage, the participants explain and sell their ideas to the others. Individuals vote based on the measurable challenge, the predefined judging criteria, and their own interest and passion.

It is important to note here, while only five to seven emerge as the key themes from the masses of pitches, the ideas that weren't chosen can still be used after the event. Most of these other ideas are shared with cross-functional teams and incorporated into other initiatives ongoing. It's a cornucopia of solid ideas that can spur future innovation and collaboration.

Pitch winners are announced to facilitate the next stage: **Teamup.**

### STAGE 4: Teamup

At this stage, the participants self-select teams based on their interests and expertise. The pitch leaders of the five to seven themes will use this time to recruit who they need to create the best solution. Self-selection is a powerful tool. It not only ensures that participants are interested in the idea, but also reduces any excuses when it comes to judging and decision time. Plus, it helps to alleviate the usual corporate politics, because the teams are more of a commonwealth vs. a dictated assembly. The number one rule about team formation is more than one and less than six people to a team. If the team is larger than six, then it is practically impossible to effectively collaborate and make decisions quickly. Factions form and progress is stunted.

### STAGE 5: Create

In this stage these self-selected teams get to work. They are given a packet of information with a detailed timeline of actions and lean startup guides to accomplish the goal of the working session, which is a 10-minute executive level presentation for judging and decision to solve the challenge question. They must also prepare for five minutes to answer questions about the solution from an experienced, discerning group of executives.

Initially, we leave the teams for an hour to do a brain dump of ideas around the chosen pitch idea. They throw in all their collective knowledge, data, and contacts into the mix to better shape the solution. Then they create some team structure with roles and responsibilities and establish a strict timeline of the deliverables.

During this time, the coaches and advisors are critical. They will rotate among the teams to offer advice, resources, and objective opinions. Usually, certain coaches gravitate to certain teams based on their expertise. But all the teams benefit from these advisors as they work to create their solution.

As mentioned before, we offer many tools for these teams to collaborate at Smart Speed, but this action pack serves as a guide, offering questions in need of answers. In addition to a simplified roster of key questions, a big requirement for teams is validation of their solution. *Have they contacted a stakeholder, a customer, a partner? Have they run it by the operations team or the business units? What proof do they have this will work?* Part of the judging criteria always includes a validation element. This ensures that the teams properly vet their solution before presenting their findings and recommendations to the judges.

*Are you thinking so what? Isn't this what organizations do already?* Not really. Today, organizations have a gluttonous, linear process with many false starts, stops, and conflicting agendas, with no sense of urgency or transparency. "Most of your innovation is hiding in plain sight; you are institutionally blinded by your legacy systems and culture." This method allows everyone to see there is another way to delivering innovation in a more democratic and streamlined way. It ensures enough due diligence to mitigate risk, but without all the bureaucracy and normal business log jams.

**STAGE 6: Present**

Then, *it's on like Donkey Kong,* as I like to say. Teams present for 10 minutes, with a 5-minute question and answer session from the executive panel of judges, who have previously committed to resource the winning plan. Just like the pitch round, these are timed to the second. This facilitates fairness and equality, but more importantly, requires teams to be concise in their presentation. Judges have scoring sheets based on the pre-defined judging criteria that everyone has been using as a guide.

> "Most of your innovation is hiding in plain sight; you are institutionally blinded by your legacy systems and culture."

Using the scoring sheets and a facilitated discussion, the judges select the winning presentation in which to invest and move forward. Meanwhile, all the participants select their favorite solution as the 'people's choice.' It's interesting that in 100% of the cases, the judges and the people's choice selection are never the same. The best part of this discrepancy is that organizations end up selecting both of the solutions to implement, which doubles the value of the experience and the outcome.

The winners are announced along with some fun superlative awards for various participants, like pitch winners and other event awards. These awards aren't big fat cash prizes, instead they are playful bragging rights and silly toys. This is followed by an after party to celebrate the win, the experience, and the innovation efforts. The participants continue the conversations throughout the evening, sharing ideas and collaborating off the clock. You have just fostered the envied startup culture and collective spirit that will permeate the status-quo-naysaying-can't-be-done attitude that stifles innovation within the enterprise. Your employees, subject matter experts and leaders have been exposed to a different system. More importantly, they have been successful in doing it. They now know how to usher impactful innovation at Smart Speed. It's a seed, it's a start, and it's the only way to start a movement to transform the enterprise from the inside out.

## STAGE 7: Follow Up

A Certified Smart Speed Solutionator wraps the event up with a summary with fun photos and a listing of all the flash pitch ideas, in an easy to collaborate and share format. Plus, the Smart Speed Solutionator sets up the 30-day, 60-day and 90-day check-in sessions with a detailed task list to complete before each meeting to ensure progress is made on the one or two selected presentations. This stage holds everyone accountable. It prevents the usual drop off from other facilitated sessions or consulting engagements. In addition, all participants receive *Weekly Zings* or weekly innovation challenges in their inbox to help them bring back the innovative culture to the office after the event. They are like booster shots to strengthen the immunity to business-as-usual.

After the teams create the executable project plans during the 90 days of follow up, the organization typically runs a pilot of the solution. The adoption is fast tracked because so many employee champions organically influence their peers in the organization, and they have already validated the solution, which helps overcome the usual objections to change and innovation.

Then the Smart Speed Solutionator schedules a 365-day check-in to review the results, return on investment, key learnings, and best practices.

That's the process to deliver at Smart Speed. In order to reach the Smart Speed status, this is not a one-and-done activity. This is a scalable and repeatable process that transforms business-as-usual behaviors into accelerated innovative and ongoing change. It is only through successful practice over time that you can transform your organization into a more INTRApreneurial culture, for the long haul. It's the only way to fulfill your Leadovator mission — creating a systemic yet fluid business ecosystem, powered by trusted talented people ready to adapt, and deliver at speed.

*Now, what should you do?*

Shamelessly, I would say hire a Certified Smart Speed Facilitator from 48 Innovate today and get started. But if you aren't convinced or ready to commit to this yet, there are a few things you can do to prepare for the transition to systemic innovation through the Smart Speed Method.

**Three Actions to Ignite this employee-driven process and begin the transition to Smart Speed:**

1. **Create space.** Daily operations are a must for a business to run, but that often leaves no time or energy for ideas, innovation, or creativity. And today your talent is running on fumes. If you want to do something, you must focus on it. Just like learning to ride a bike, you must dedicate time to learn and practice to master the skill. The same goes for innovation. Employees must have dedicated time to think, collaborate, and share with others to unearth the next BIG idea. Consider automating low-value tasks or outsourcing them to create room for innovation to emerge and flourish. Stop wasting all your talent's energy on the day-to-day, instead dedicate some time to innovation; it's the only way.

2. **Institute a consistent process.** Process seems so counter to innovation. It's controlled; it's predictable; it's repeatable and it's scalable. These are not inherent traits of creativity or innovation, right? Not for innovation itself, but you must have an intentional method to foster innovation as a *habit*.

   Don't overlook the "consistent" part of this action. This process must be repeated. It must be predictable, i.e., it happens annually, quarterly, or monthly. Employees need to rely on it. It channels random idea generation, curbs frustration and cynicism, and allows a gentle refocus on daily operations the rest of the work time because of the promise of an established forum for innovation and creativity. This consistent process weaves innovation into the fabric of your organization's culture without sacrificing the immediate operational needs of the business.

3. **Execute and promote success.** This is the big AHA! The money shot. The actions that drive culture, sustainability, and ultimately your organization's competitive advantage. Once the process to discover internal innovation is complete, then it's the execution of that BIG idea that matters. It's what makes the uncomfortable, challenging part of innovation, worth it. Success breeds success. Once you deliver a successful, quantifiable employee-driven innovation within an organization, next you must promote it. It is the guidepost that will drive the future. Showcase how the risk paid off. Tout how your employees made it happen. And then wash, rinse, and repeat.

These three actions will deliver the meaning and impact those esteemed millennials and Gen Fluxers demand. It will allow you to lead an enterprise transformation others will only dream about. It will identify and develop INTRApreneurs taking on more responsibility and decision making, relieving the business log jams and endless nights of insomnia from the relentless pressure of growth and advancement. It's the beginning of the next generation enterprise that all others will rip and duplicate. It's the path to Smart Speed. Leadovators, mount up!

# THE Weekly ZING

## Your Innovation Challenge
## Cutting Room Floor

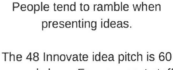

People tend to ramble when presenting ideas.

The 48 Innovate idea pitch is 60 seconds long. For your next staff meeting, set aside 60 seconds for a team member to pitch their best innovative idea for growth.

Share this recipe with the team before to help them prepare – why + idea + expected outcome = pitch.

One Up It: Make this idea pitch a part of every staff meeting moving forward. Have the team vote if you should pursue or not. Then take action.

Share your 60-second pitch with @48Innovate use #cuttingroomfloor.

# Part 2

# Complete: The Knowledge is in Your hands — Locked and Loaded to Lead *The Innovation Revolution*

Don't turn away from the ugliness of the truth. There is another way. You must stop the busywork and buzzword bingo to restore the trust and the resources you need for the innovation transformation. It's a mind shift to strategic agility. It's a direction ... not a destination. It takes patience and practice to undo the usual. It takes courage. It takes profound leadership. All of which you have. You are a Leadovator and it's all up to you.

The Smart Speed Method is a reconfiguration of what you already know and do, activated by authentic employee engagement to skip the slow corporate dance and deliver innovation and results continuously, and at speed. It is an experiential practice that offers safe passage outside the lines of business-as-usual. You are ready to lead *The Innovation Revolution*. You got this. Let's go!

**Next up:**

Find your guided path forward with an action plan to help you revamp, retool, and reform business-as-usual and bravely lead *The Innovation Revolution* inside the enterprise.

Before the next page turn, you must prepare for action.

- UPWARD SALUTE POSE -

Stretch before you pull a muscle. Instantly rejuvenate and let the blood flow with this Upward Salute Pose, *Urdhva Hastasana (OORD-vah hahs-TAHS-uh-nuh)*. Hold this pose for 5 deep breaths.

In three recent studies, stretching proved to increase memory function and thinking clarity. In her book "Stretching," Suzanne Martin, a physical therapist, likens stretching to a neurological panacea.[37] Let the floodgates open with this stretch to prepare you for your noble mission ahead.

---

[37] *http://healthyliving.azcentral.com/neurologic-advantage-actively-stretching-13704.html*

## A Special Bonus from Melissa

With your copy of *The Innovation Revolution*, you are ready to inject the nimble, entrepreneurial spirit **back** into the enterprise with the genius hiding in plain sight.

Armed with proof of the complexity and intensity you face day-to-day, you know where to start, and where you must go. You are empowered to stand up and say NO to all that is impeding your path forward. AND, you are loaded with tools to make it happen.

For your courage to lead against business-as-usual, you deserve a little something special.

Here is my bonus gift for you:

- Discover your own hidden genius and ensure success with the digital workbook, **Activate Your Hidden Genius: 7 Surefire Actions to Ignite *The Innovation Revolution***
- Explore walking outside the lines and help make it stick with **The Weekly Zing**, an annual email subscription of weekly mini innovation exercises
- Take a simple **Three Little Orgs Innovation Assessment** to reveal your organization's innovation status and inform your next move

Go to http://innovationrevolutionbook.com/signup to access your bonus material.

Enjoy the ride in the driver's seat for your high speed, high impact journey to save the enterprise.

*It's on like Donkey Kong!*

Melissa

# Part 3

# A Guided Path Forward

Within the pages in this book so far, you have been armed with macro trends, insider stories, and quick tips to begin the journey to systemic innovation within your enterprise, powered by INTRApreneur employees. You have the method and mindset to lead *The Innovation Revolution* to save your enterprise. The most daunting task is straight ahead – the transition.

The transition is moving from the current sloth's pace of business-as-usual and empty innovation promises, to reinvent yourself, empower your employees, and evolve your organization to deliver results at Smart Speed.

Just like a jet needs runway lights to guide its takeoff and landing, you too, need a guided path forward. Discover jumpstart actions to help you quickly revamp, retool, and reform business-as-usual to dominate in today's dynamic rapid hyper-connected environment.

In the chapters ahead, you will discover real-live-no-jive get-it-done advice from research, practitioners, field tests, and experience. Hold on, you are getting ready to find the answers you seek to ride the wave of innovation success, with just a flip of a page.

- POWER POSE -

Take a deep breath and assume your best power pose to begin your *Innovation Revolution* journey.

# Chapter 10

# Prepare for the New Leadership Era of Empathy

*"The most basic of all human needs is the need to understand
and to be understood."*
— *Ralph Nichols*

Promise of the Chapter:

- Introduce human-centered business and the Era of Empathy.
- Review a brief history of management and its evolution leading to this next era.
- Empower you with empathy to lead *The Innovation Revolution*.

Flashback to PART ONE of this book:

- Millennials and Gen Fluxers are demanding respect, autonomy and meaning, combined with an emerging Big Quit trend to exclaim those demands.
- Proliferation of technology combined with obsessive risk management are destroying humanity and innovation within the enterprise.
- Lean startup methodologies with built-in customer empathy and relevance are ushering in millions of startups, kicking ass and taking names.
- This is your 21st century leadership reality — information overload, uber complex, and accelerated pace of change and intense pressure of growth and results with overextended resources, and outdated, dysfunctional internal processes and systems

These realities drive the undeniable need to deliver a constant stream of value, creating innovation from within the enterprise. In order to ensure the value to customers and to rely on the talent and resources you have, and lead *The Innovation Revolution*, it's time to embrace a new era in leadership and management: The Era of Empathy.

Empathy is the only way to overcome the loss of humanity in the enterprise.

*It's the grounding force to prevail over the evils of the corporate underbelly and buzzwords gone bad.*

*It's the only way to cultivate a trusting environment where co-creation among the complex matrix of stakeholders inside and out can exist and at speed and with confidence.*

*It's the fuel to usher in Smart Speed as the new normal. Prepare to lead the shift.*

The notion of a human-centered business is still fairly new. *Weird huh? Why isn't the human a top priority? Aren't humans the ones who buy things? Create things?* We discussed this loss of humanity in Part One of this book and now it's time to face the music, stop crushing all your potential, and discover the antidote.

For years, management has been focused on one thing — driving results no matter the cost to your employees, or the world for that matter ... but that's changing. (Thank goodness!) Over the last few years, leaders have started to recognize the importance of connecting with their employees, their partners, and customers, who are humans, by the way, on both a professional and personal level.

Connection is vital. And the jet fuel for connection is empathy. Leaders can unleash results by simply understanding employees' work styles and motivations. Have employees apply this same notion to understanding customer and stakeholder experiences, too. These insights are the key to unlocking value, competitive advantage, and operationalizing innovation within the enterprise.

**Here is an example of how the marketplace demonstrates this demand for empathy experience from every professional regardless of title:**

Today, among the most highly sought professionals are user experience (UX) designers. Their top skill is translating user empathy and understanding into a designed experience for a service, product, or other applications. The UX professionals observe and articulate how the users think, feel, say, and do, then apply insights and advantages to propel the outcome forward. Further proof of this demand for more user empathy is the popularity of concepts like design thinking, empathy maps, and customer journey maps. These are all proof points for the need to weave empathy-driven practices into your daily operations — for your employees, stakeholders, and customers.

*Do your organizational operations and culture factor in empathy? Empathy for employees, stakeholders, partners or customers?* If not, that is a fundamental root cause impeding the transformation to Smart Speed and systemic innovation.

A simple place to start: Make employee ideas, voices, and actions matter through connection and empathy. Respect and trust are cornerstones to creating a productive collaborative environment. You must channel your inner Aretha Franklin and "R-E-S-P-E-C-T," and find out what it all means to your team. That's empathy activated ... the magic fairy dust to make the Smart Speed Method work and lead *The Innovation Revolution* to deliver systemic innovation within the enterprise. It's an empathetic leader who allows employees to explore and execute their version of the outcome, with a little guidance and steering along the way. It's the responsibility of a Leadovator. It's new. It's real. It's been a long time coming.

A mini history lesson helps explain the path to the Era of Empathy. I'm borrowing from Columbia Business School Professor Rita Gunther McGrath, who laid out the evolution of management in a 2014 article for the Harvard Business Review.[38] *(Thanks Rita, you rock!)*

**Management: A VERY Brief History**

1. **Pre-Industrial Revolution:** Management was just for churches, military, and a few domestic endeavors, and based mainly on slave labor.

2. **Industrial Revolution, Early 1900s**: One of the first management specialists, Peter Drucker, introduced the now famous notion of the *knowledge worker*. He said that workers' value wasn't created just by their production of goods or execution of tasks, but also by their use of information,

---

[38] *https://hbr.org/2014/07/managements-three-eras-a-brief-history/*

which challenged all that organizations know about the proper relationships between managers and subordinates.

Good ole Albert Einstein eloquently summarized this transition when he said, "The intuitive mind is a sacred gift and the rational mind is a faithful servant. We have created a society that honors the servant and has forgotten the gift."

3. **Mid-twentieth Century**: This period ushered a proliferation of management theories and gave rise to the expert age, where there were specialists with advanced education to tackle complex issues or innovations. This led to the rise of management consulting firms and outsourcing. It was studded with all sorts of management trends, including the precursor to the waterfall project management model and continuous improvement methods like Six Sigma.

4. **Twentieth Century and Beyond:** A new era in management has been brewing with the rise of emotional intelligence and emphasis on employee engagement, which some are calling the Era of Empathy. It's evident through the unprecedented focus on user, customer, or employee experience. Only through understanding what your audience experiences, feels, and does can you create sustained value. The role of leaders in management today is one of coaching, community building, and co-creating vs. the command and control of times past.

   *What does leadership and management look like when work is done through networks instead of lines of command?* "Work" itself is tinged with emotions, and individual leaders are responsible for creating and nurturing communities for those who work for and with them.

   *If what is demanded of leaders today is empathy, then we must ask: what new roles and organizational structures make sense? How should performance management be approached? What does it take for a leader to function as a "pillar" and how should the next generation of leader be taught?* Combine that new "grey" dynamic with the pressure of growth at speed and outdated internal operations, and no wonder you feel like you are losing your mind.

## Here is a simple theme:

### An Empathetic Leader Nourishes an Environment of Innovation and Change

The new leader, a.k.a. Leadovator, must create an environment that nourishes innovation, where the job is to assist employees to execute their ideas among an environment of constant change and uncertainty. This leader embraces key themes from design thinking, like empathy, experimenting, and prototyping.

### Three Skills a Leadovator must master to thrive in today's complex Era of Empathy and lead *The Innovation Revolution*:

1. Emotional intelligence;
2. Community creation and management within the matrix;
3. Empowerment among the matrix and especially employees.

**1. EMOTIONAL INTELLIGENCE** within themselves, their team, their organization, their partners, and even their customers. It's a matrix. It's complex. And, it is moving at light speed. One-up that with a side of user experience, emphasizing the end user actions and reactions at every stage of development and delivery.

This community creation and management entails the ability to facilitate connections among direct reports, adjacent departments, up and down the hierarchy, and external stakeholders too; all of which are globally dispersed and loaded with varied motivations and goals. The research from Dr. Travis Bradberry's Emotional Intelligence 2.0 book, revealed a peculiar finding that people with average IQs, but high EQs, outperformed 70% of the time than those with just high IQs. His study proved that emotional intelligence while less measureable and tangible is an essential characteristic of high performers.[39]

### Five Bullet-Proof Steps to beef up your EQ or Emotional Intelligence:

**Step 1: Increase your emotional vocabulary.** It's not just important to know that there are negative or "bad" feelings or emotions within yourself or others. You must be able to determine what those emotions are and descriptively label them. Are they frustrated, angry or irritated? What is the real source of these emotions and what can you do to manage them? Awareness of these emotions is step one, and then constructively labeling them and investigating their cause is the only way to manage.

---

[39] http://www.inc.com/travis-bradberry/are-you-emotionally-intelligent-here-s-how-to-know-for-sure.html

**Step 2: Be actively curious**. Curiosity of people, their motivations, reactions, and goals is imperative to drive progress. Seek out new interactions with a diverse set of people, not just ones on your team, in your country, or within your business ecosystem. Go to an event that has nothing to do with your normal interests or interactions. Seek out new adventures to meet and get to know different people and their stories. There are plenty of diverse experiences on sites like Meetup.com. Pick one new event a quarter to attend. The next time you are at a conference, instead of connecting with your same crew, challenge yourself to sit at a table or row where you do not know anyone. Set a goal to meet a new person at each session and get to know them — why are they here, what interests them, and who they are. Curiosity is the pathway to knowledge, and application of that knowledge is power.

**Step 3: Know yourself — emotional strengths and weaknesses inventory**. We've heard this from every career advisor on the planet — discover your strengths and weaknesses. But this step has a bit of nuance. It's not just strengths and weaknesses on a skill level, but on an emotional level and how you interact with others. What are your own emotional hot buttons? In what situations do you shine? Are you a masterful networker or do you dive deep to get to know people beyond the LinkedIn contact level? Knowing your own emotional strengths and weaknesses is the only way to manage your interaction with others.

**Step 4: Stop avalanching and learn to let go**. *Have you ever just piled on? When something bad happens at work or home, instead of just dealing with that incident in isolation, you add up everything that has gone wrong within the week, month or year?* That is what I call avalanching, where we pile on all the negative or unexpected things happening in our lives, both at work and play. If you pile on too high, you are headed for a crash. STOP. Deal with one situation at a time and then let it go. Keeping an inventory of the injustices or bad incidents in your life doesn't do anything for you. You end up transferring all that negativity to the people around you and that is no way to lead teams into greatness. It is a sunk cost. Nothing can change it and wallowing in it will only suck up your energy meant for something else.

Recognize the avalanche. Stop piling on. Breathe. Lead on with wisdom. Simple actions to a more powerful you.

**Step 5: Lead with gratitude**. A recent study from University of California, Davis, discovered that people who have an attitude of gratitude reduced the stress hormone cortisol by 23% in some cases.[40] The science doesn't lie, but more important than less stress is its effect on our mood and overall physical well-being. It takes more than mental prowess to lead change and innovation. It takes physical and energetic fortitude. Leading with gratitude is a contagious mindset and spreads like Kudzu (In case you have never heard that one, Kudzu is a plant that grows a foot a day in the southern United States). It boosts positivity and creativity. Gratitude is the antidote to the toxic. It diffuses people and escalating situations. It provides much needed perspective when things are so close. Being thankful isn't just a nice to do, it is imperative to withstand the barrage of complex warp speed challenges faced every day.

Leading with gratitude sounds simple enough. *Just be thankful for what you have and who you are, right?* Sometimes that simple truth fades. Cultivating a habit to be grateful takes routine and discipline.

Every morning while you are in shower, say out loud what you are grateful for. It can be as simple as, "I am grateful for this warm, clean shower."

Incorporate this exercise within your team, by starting or closing each staff meeting with the team sharing something they are grateful for. It sounds hokey, but if you don't practice, it won't stick.

Take these five steps to be more emotionally intelligent and observe the tone, energy, and environment transform. It's easy to get busy and dismiss the feelings and emotions of others, but those others are the powerful force you need to launch new innovative initiatives consistently, and at Smart Speed.

**2. COMMUNITY CREATION AND MANAGEMENT WITHIN THE MATRIX.** Facilitate connections among direct reports, adjacent departments, up and down the hierarchy, and external stakeholders too, all of whom are globally dispersed and loaded with varied motivations and goals.

The matrix isn't some reference of the cult-followed movie trilogy starring Keanu Reeves. No, it's the interconnected people that support the very existence of your business. It's the employees that faithfully serve your customers day in and day out. It's the suppliers and vendors that you work with

---

[40] *http://www.ucdmc.ucdavis.edu/welcome/features/2015-2016/11/20151125_gratitude. html*

to enable your business to deliver. It's the customers that are the lifeblood of your business.

In the past, leaders tried to create distance among all these ecosystem players in order to control, with good intentions, I am sure. Distance among these powerful, aligned forces only causes more confusion, delays, and less progress. Only by breaking down the business-as-usual barriers can organizations transform and leapfrog the competition. These connections within the matrix create the entire experience map of your business. As complex as that is to imagine, it is the simple truth. At each intersection, touch point or engagement is an opportunity to innovate, differentiate, and add value. These powerful communities are the force multiplier, the proprietary parts to your innovation engine.

*How to enable these connections to deliver without introducing more noise and complexity into the "system?"*

**Step 1: Face it.** You can no longer control the flow of information. With the introduction of the Internet and social media, information is more visible and available than ever before. The best way to begin your community-building journey is to accept that truth.

**Step 2: Embrace it**. After you have taken a few deep breaths and accepted the fact that you can't keep these people from connecting, it's time to embrace it and use it to your advantage. Understanding the experiences and interactions of your company with your matrix of stakeholders delivers on your empathy intelligence. This offers a reality check and validation points to help improve everything from your billing system to your service offering. Every interaction with your company is an opportunity to build loyalty and value. And in the era of niche markets, micro engagement and interaction, this can be the difference between market share and market fail.

**Step 3: Encourage your employees to connect with cross-functional team members, partners, and customers on projects.** Build in your project plan a validation and user reality check test before anything moves forward. Often teams use tools like empathy maps or customer journey maps to find insights and advantages. Examples of these tools, techniques, and instructions can be found with a simple Internet search. Incorporate these exercises into your next project to capture your competitive advantage through empathy and connection.

Remember, many people use systems in unique and unintended ways that can save you money or build competitive advantage. Co-creating solutions will not only improve quality, but fast track the traditional waterfall project cycle. This very idea of user validation is fundamental to the Eric Ries Build-Measure-Learn lean startup model. Yes, it's scary showing your cards before your hand is complete, but it's far worse that you lose when the winning card you need is in the hands of your ecosystem and available for play.

**Step 4: Always be giving.** The open source movement taught us the power of giving without any expectation of anything in return. The spirit of giving is one from which we all benefit. In order to cultivate an authentic, reciprocal community, it must be built on a foundation of generosity. It is that very selflessness that allows for progress to be made. Generosity breaks barriers, diffuses egos, and diminishes ulterior motives. It builds relationships, not walls. It allows creativity and collaboration to thrive. The number one rule when developing communities is always be giving.

**Step 5: Demonstrate how to connect and build social capital within the matrix.** If you want to calm that fear that someone might jeopardize a relationship unintentionally, then you must show your team and colleagues how. Take a small project and co-lead the interaction with a small loyal customer set. Don't bring in expectations and demands. Pose challenges that need to be solved and facilitate the community to solve them through low fi visual tools like giant flip charts, whiteboards, colorful Post-its, and markers. Don't jump to solutions, just figure out what is happening. Always delay judgment and criticism until later in the process. Show them how to respectfully debate and then how to decide and act. It is through your example that all the people within the matrix learn how to work together for everyone's benefit.

Next you need to teach your team how to build some street 'cred' or social capital. I always encourage people to build relationships with their celebrity stakeholders or endorsers. You know the big influencer in the community. Going big is far easier when you know what's around the corner and you have what I call an Office LeBron James in your corner. That's right: a celebrity endorser. Office Lebron is the champion who will support an idea or initiative, someone with organizational fame, like a key customer or influential leader. You must teach your employees how to identify and endear Office LeBron through connection and collaboration.

Those leaders and organizations that optimize their relationships among all the stakeholders and teach their employees to do the same will rapidly deliver innovation consistently and confidently.

**3. EMPOWERMENT AMONG THE MATRIX AND ESPECIALLY EMPLOYEES.** Empowerment comes in a variety of flavors, from tweaking an employee's idea to make it sing, or framing assignments as a problem or desired result instead of instructing how to do it. It's allowing your employees to learn through failure and succeed through experimentation. It's silencing all the naysayers and amplifying the wild and zany. It's having the courage to allow employees to work with customers or other stakeholders to create solutions that are both relevant and novel. It's the essential action to transforming the controlling dysfunctional culture and internal processes of the past into a nimble, effective system that delivers innovation consistently and at speed. It also will help lift the burden on you, as the leader, of backlogged decisions and projects necessary to successfully compete in the swift chaos of change.

**Step 1: Demonstrate faith and confidence within your employees**. It is your responsibility as a leader to demonstrate your confidence in employees by giving them autonomy and authority. You must let go your need to control and micro manage and give your team space to explore and experiment. Even when they aren't around, you are the one who sets the tone with peers and other leaders. Those innocent eye rolls at conferences when the keynote challenges you to trust your employees. The sighs of frustration when something fails or misses the mark. No one, including yourself, is perfect. People will rise to the level to which you allow them. It is up to you to have faith and confidence in each employee and provide them the opportunity and support to excel.

You are the only one who can do it. Lead and your team will follow with surprise, delight, and a can of whoopass in their pocket.

**Step 2: Put on your whistle and get ready to coach.** Coaching isn't for little league anymore, oh no. The new era of empathy requires more of a coach than a commander. It is the "ask," not the "tell." You must guide your employees, not dictate. The knowledge worker of today is educated, intelligent, and insightful. Nothing can be accomplished solo, nothing outstanding that is. It's using stories and examples from your past to explain and demonstrate. You must set expectations, pose challenges not tasks, and give them freedom to experiment, learn and achieve, while you are on the sidelines influencing along the way. It takes restraint, don't underestimate that. It's in the moment, it's ongoing, and it's the new normal.

**Step 3: Diffuse toxic people.** It is your role as a leader to diffuse the negative nellys, the it's-always-been-done-that-way, it-will-never-work, we-have-tried-that-before people in your matrix. Whether it is your employees, your peers, or bully customers, you must lead with opportunity and confidence and demonstrate your support for your team. Too often the toxic comments come from within and sometimes from outside, but there is no place for that negativity in the world of innovation and results. That toxic can't-do attitude is enemy number one on your quest to operationalize innovation in the enterprise. The only way to allow ideas to flourish is ensure a trusting and open environment. You must hold the line and delay criticism and judgment during brainstorming. You must teach the negative ones how to build with the famous improv concept "yes, and" instead of "but, no." Teach your employees how to ask clarifying questions or phrase specific roadblocks and obstacles instead of "dissing" the idea all together. That is how constructive debate can transform a seed idea into a brilliant plan. And new ideas, trust, and confidence are the walls that complete the hall of **empowerment.**

**Step 4: Cultivate patience.** Shit happens. It's true. Sometimes there are riffs and the universe is out of balance. Discord is a natural outcome to debate. Some people don't get along. Humans have been fighting since the beginning of time. It's your job to demonstrate patience when things don't go your way and impart that skill on to your team and others you influence to empower the whole community. Patience is hard when you are overextended and overwhelmed by the fierce need for a quick solution or answer. Patience is the ultimate gift. When diverse people come together on a project or goal, it is important that the team tempers its passion with patience to develop the best possible solution. I don't know many entrepreneurs who are naturally patient, but they will be the first to tell you the power that comes from cultivating that skill.

You have to be able to see people. You have to be able to imagine what their world is like outside the office. In order to empower, you have to empathize and share your strength to boost theirs. Patience is fundamental to empowerment, as challenging as it is to master. You can't steadily deliver excellence without it.

Master these steps and impart their wisdom on your matrix and empowerment will be right behind. The Era of Empathy has arrived. Taking these simple steps will prepare you for this new era and prepare you to lead *The Innovation Revolution* charge.

# Chapter 11

## Many-Faced Leadovator

*"You must be shapeless, formless, like water. When you pour water in a cup, it becomes the cup. When you pour water in a bottle, it becomes the bottle. When you pour water in a teapot, it becomes the teapot. Water can drip and it can crash. Become like water my friend."*

— *Bruce Lee*

Promise of the Chapter:

- Offer situation-based applications of Leadovator responses to transform the enterprise.
- Challenge traditional methods that must evolve to operationalize innovation in the enterprise.
- Develop new Leadovator skills to lead *The Innovation Revolution*.

Now it's time to put your empathy skills to the test. Remember way back in Part One when you took the leader assessment? Good. That's where we will start.

If you watched the popular HBO series *Game of Thrones*, you may remember the storyline of the *Many-Faced God*. It was a character that could literally transform itself into other people. Think of this exercise as something similar, just not as creepy. You are channeling other personas when a situation requires it. Don't **over rotate** and pretend to be someone you are not, but consider embracing these skills and attitudes in certain situations.

## Here is a refresher of the leader archetypes:

| Leader Attitude Archetypes | Common Attitudes and Actions |
|---|---|
| Pleaser | Embraces empathy, seeks approval of others, finds it difficult to express true feelings and thoughts, fears rejection |
| Explorer | Embraces uncertainty, acts selflessly to do the right thing, engages in dialogue not debates |
| Imperialist | Delivers no matter what, uses I/Me/My frequently, dislikes bad news, strives to be in charge |

And here are the top aptitudes by leader type we reviewed before. As you can see, each of the archetypes have valuable strengths that will come in handy as you evolve and lead *The Innovation Revolution*.

| Top Pleaser Aptitudes | Top Explorer Aptitudes | Top Imperialist Aptitudes | Top Leadovator Aptitudes |
|---|---|---|---|
| Management by objective | Recognizes his/ her limitations | Delegation | Digital fluent |
| Project management | Ability to let go, adapt | Recruiting | Analysis |
| Consensus-building | Prioritizes experimentation and learning | Developing Key Performance Indicators (KPI)/metrics | Problem solving |
| Ethics | Embraces uncertainty and ambiguity | Providing direction | Resource management across the matrix of stakeholders |
| Reporting | Collaborative | Find and leverage quick wins | Clear communication despite imperfect information and ambiguity |

As explained, yet bears mentioning again here, each of those characteristics come in handy, depending on the circumstances. This Many-Faced This Many-Faced Leadovator exercise is all about developing your weaker side and learning when is the best time to use those personas as you lead your team and organization through *The Innovation Revolution*. It takes that empathy muscle to understand how to apply the qualities and skills of the *Pleaser, Imperialist*, and the *Explorer* when the situation warrants, at speed and with confidence. You will have to purposely decide to choose the alternate response, and it **will** feel unnatural at first. According to Charles Duhigg, author of *The Power of Habit*, habit behaviors are traced to a part of the brain called the basal ganglia — a portion of the brain associated with emotions, patterns, and memories. Decisions, on the other hand, are made in the prefrontal cortex, which is a completely different area. When a behavior becomes habit, we stop using our decision-making skills and instead function on auto-pilot. Therefore, breaking a bad habit and building a new habit not only requires us to make active decisions, it will *feel* wrong. Your brain will resist the change in favor of what it has been programmed to do.[41] Now we aren't talking about breaking a bad habit necessarily, but we are choosing to take a different approach and a better alternative. It's good to set your expectations on the not-so-normal-feeling you will experience initially. Recognizing the situation and choosing the optimal response is strategic agility in motion powered by empathy.

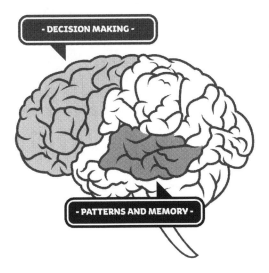

---

[41] *https://www.amazon.com/Power-Habit-What-Life-Business/dp/081298160X*

There are common organizational situations that you will encounter as you lead *The Innovation Revolution* matched with the optimal response and applicable leader archetype and aptitudes needed to deliver. Note that no situation is clear cut because these are complex scenarios and require a hybrid or complex response to match them. The Leadovator aptitudes are essential as you lead your organization's transition from its old school ways to the new normal.

> "It's good to set your expectations on the not-so-normal-feeling you will experience initially. Recognizing the situation and choosing the optimal response is strategic agility in motion powered by empathy."

**Ten Most Common Situations a leader experiences and the optimal response in this *Innovation Revolution*:**

**Situation 1: Budget Cuts, Layoffs, and Hard Times.** Every organization encounters these at least once in their lifetime. Budget cuts and layoffs are not pleasant, but rather common these days. There are always lean times if your organization is lucky enough to make it for the long haul.

*Optimal Response:* This situation requires a hybrid approach based on audience. When you are at the negotiating table for budget cuts or layoffs with your peers or others, fighting for resources, you must understand that the knee-jerk response of organizations is to halt the innovative. Organizations hunker down in these hard times. It is important that you, as a visionary leader, are vigilant in future-proofing the organization, because these hard times won't last forever. You want to first embrace the take charge attitude and metrics acumen of the *Imperialist*. You want to defend as much turf as you can to persevere the innovation needed to pull your organization out of the hole.

When dealing with your team, you will want to embrace the *Pleaser* attitude of empathy and understanding. It's a way you and your team can deal with the loss of either funding or people. You want to reevaluate your objectives in the face of these changes and manage them to deliver despite the loss. Don't forget to relentlessly follow the highest ethical compass during the transition to keep everyone above board and out of court.

This one is tough. But it takes a 1-2 punch to persevere until the good times. And you absolutely must lead with your Leadovator skills to insist that innovation isn't a nice-to-have, but the key to the upswing in the uber-competitive, fast paced environment of today.

**Situation 2: Annual Planning.** Every year, this spins every leader in a whirlwind. In the middle of delivering on the "what is right in front of you," you are asked to yank out your crystal ball and decide what to plan for the future. Strategic planning is the process where leaders get together, review the historical data and industry trends with the forecast of new products, services or delivery mechanisms, and decide next year's annual goals, objectives, organization structure, and operational plans to make it all happen. Strategic planning should be grounded in proper analysis and measured response to minimize major disruption to the business and false knee-jerk reactions; however, it can't blindly ignore the speed and complexity in which customers' needs shift and markets move.

*Optimal Response:* This is when you want the hybrid response from the *Imperialist* and the *Explorer*. This offers your metrics discipline of the Imperialist nuanced with the adaptability and inclusiveness of the *Explorer* to look beyond the numbers or the titles and bring in others below the senior management ranks into the fold for field insights and a reality check. Add in the Leadovator skills and you have a future-proof combination that will cause a little wrestling, but will spit out a viable strategic plan to drive killer results.

> *A Harvard study found that annual planning cycles and formal strategic planning has been proven to not benefit the company in that it takes too long to make decisions, hence they are irrelevant once they are made.[42] You may want to consider transforming your annual planning cycles for more iterative strategy sprints. In this fast-paced change dynamic, too often plans and decisions are already irrelevant by the time they are approved. You don't want to cause disruptive changes, but you do need to embrace a more strategic, agile approach where you use these traditional planning cycles to decide on direction, but then create planning sprints to tweak closer to real-time to address market dynamics.*

---

[42] *https://hbr.org/2006/01/stop-making-plans-start-making-decisions*

**Situation 3: Priority Shifts and Organization Restructure.** Organizations are constantly evolving and, therefore, priorities will shift. As a natural byproduct of those shifts come change in organizational structures, meaning, who reports to who directly or indirectly. Investments of budget and resources follow the highest priorities and opportunities, so when one group shrinks, another will grow.

> *While commonplace, researchers at Harvard found that the restructuring that happens in large enterprises almost annually does nothing to improve resource allocation or fast track decision-making. Customers don't care how you are organized; they require a seamless experience, where the wizard is always hidden behind the curtain. Plus, the interconnectedness of people and solutions tangle the traditional linear reporting structures like last year's holiday lights pulled from the attic. It would be far more effective for leaders to master managing the matrix of stakeholders and people resources indirectly and based on problem statements and skill requirements to deliver versus traditional arbitrary departments. This sort of evolution would require incredible trust throughout the organization.*

*Optimal Response:* You must handle this with confidence, empathy, and adaptability; hence, you need to be all three leader archetypes for this one. Change creates uncertainty which fuels fear, rumors, and lots of unproductive actions among the layers within the whole organization.

Sometimes leaders land-grab for power and resources, employees overreact by busywork disguised as value-delivering activities. You need the "it's done, let's move on" attitude of the *Imperialist,* balanced by the empathic concern and understanding of the *Pleaser,* combined with the buy-in building collaborator of the Explorer to rally everyone around the change through advice and insight among employees in order to usher the best transition. You need to instill confidence in every layer of the organization and position this as normal flexibility to the market.

Priority shifts and restructure will become more commonly delivered at faster speeds, and you need to embrace all three of these leader archetypes to help your organization adopt this as the new normal. Building structures with flexibility allows for an agile and market-driven organization. This is the future *The Innovation Revolution* prepares us all for.

**Situation 4: Competitive Threats.** If you don't have any competition, you are either dead as an organization or playing the ostrich role with your head in the sand, because they are everywhere. Competition has increased in complexity almost beyond comprehension. You have direct competitors, frenemies, adjacent and vertical ones. Competition is everywhere. Often, throughout time, you have a few really hitting you hard, persuading your consumers to switch or stealing your new prospects. These become a most wanted lineup. You have takeout programs, battle cards, and strike teams to focus on these painful few.

*Optimal Response:* Another combo approach is warranted to meet this challenge. The trifecta will position the best response: *Pleaser, Imperialist,* and *Explorer,* wrapped into one competition-crushing leader.

Your *Pleaser* will help develop meaningful, relevant takeout programs by using the empathy skill. Understand the experiences throughout the customer delivery chain and apply your best differentiated competences to meet the competitive threat.

Your *Explorer* will easily let go of the old ways of doing things and quickly adapt to meet the new normal. Their collaborative nature will quickly take baseline programs and battle cards and tweak to meet geographical and vertical nuance in the marketplace.

Your *Imperialist* will leverage that quick win to show examples to everyone when these competitive tactics are working and when they aren't. They will share these widely so others can R&D, *rip and duplicate*, to create a tidal wave of success. And they will fight for more resources where the threat is fiercest to ensure victory.

**Situation 5: Internal Turf Wars.** Don't deny it because it is ugly. It happens everywhere. Power is seductive and organizational compensation models only sweeten the pot. The more resources you control, often the more money you make. Internal turf wars are normal. I would argue these are more frequent than in times past, because they usually emerge in times of transition or change. When leaders fight for control and power amongst themselves, you have an internal turf war that destructs and destroys.

*Optimal Response:* Your *Explorer* with Leadovator skills and attitudes is the best leader archetype to change this dynamic for the new future. Change will only increase in frequency and complexity. Leaders must all learn how to let go of the counter-productive turf wars and embrace this notion of indirect and direct management resources. Understand that their employees, budgets, and systems are flexible to meet the changing needs of customers and the market. Understand that direct control is shortsighted. Only by influencing and leveraging all resources inside, outside, and around, can the path to power and progress be created.

To set the example of open thinking, shared resources, and a common mission to adapt to bring exponential more value than your competitors is the path forward; not petty pretend power games that waste precious time, resources, and energy. Only through shared success will organizations win.

**Situation 6: Leadership Changes.** CxOs, VPs, SVPs, and directors change positions. It happens. It's not necessarily bad, it just is. Handling these changes will be critical to ensure stability and confidence, as well as adapt to styles and priorities. The bigger and more public an organization is, the more challenging this situation becomes because of speculation and a complete lack of direct control of noise outside the organization.

*Optimal Response:* Depending on what level of change and how public it is, it is important to have a response plan, inside and out. It's critical to be transparent yet directive. Frequency of communication inside and outside of the organization will be essential to prevent distracting rumors or disruption to the business.

Your *Pleaser* manager takes the lead to understand how this affects employees' experience through empathy. The *Imperialist* helps maintain confidence and control with the focus on execution during the transition. The *Explorer* helps position the opportunities that come with this kind of change and can help inform the next hire through the optimal changes to implement with this unforeseen transition.

In addition to these leader traits to manage and optimize the leadership change, it is essential that the new leader get to know the organization and its people. They must immediately introduce themselves and establish a connection. Communication should be clear, transparent, and frequent to keep the organization focused.

**Situation 7: Inheriting a Team or Employees.** This scenario happens if you start a new job or through consolidation or restructure. Don't underestimate the fear, doubt, and uncertainty felt on both sides of the equation. Similar to the leadership change situation, it is critical to connect early and communicate often.

*Optimal Response:* The best place to start is with the empathy skills and goal setting of the *Pleaser*. This allows you to share who you are and connect to establish trust early on. Following this first introduction, you will want to set the *Explorer's* tone of adaptation and experimentation as the overarching engagement model. Once you have built understanding and trust and collaborated on priorities and go forward plan, you bring in the Imperialist to rally to quick wins you all can celebrate and build on.

This is your biggest opportunity to set up the best environment for innovation. It's your chance to identify which employees are INTRApreneurs who can swing the momentum toward a more nimble, adaptable innovation delivery organization. Don't dismiss or waste this opportunity.

**Situation 8: Missed Goals or Numbers.** Ugh, missing your goals as a team sucks. There is no other way to put it. The reasons behind the miss could be outside or inside your control, but no matter what, it will be received negatively and you must stop the darkness of the miss from spreading.

*Optimal Response:* You first must seek to understand why this happened. The *Imperialist* would bring an objective numbers-based view. The *Pleaser* would sift out the subtleties within the team and beyond. The *Explorer* would invite the team to discuss, diagnose, and learn from the loss.

After this assessment, it is critical to get your story straight from *why* to *how* it will be remedied. You must acknowledge both the uncontrollable and the controllable to create a realistic path forward. All three leader types combined can confidently manage this situation up, down, and around the ecosystem. The *Pleaser* could rally the team to overcome, the *Explorer* can creatively make this a learning opportunity and introduce changes organically, and the *Imperialist* would move swiftly to get the next win to show progress and change.

While it is a loss plain and simple, a Leadovator would use this opportunity as a way to introduce new frameworks to experiment with new solutions. You must manage the disappointment, fear, and uncertainty with confidence and support to overcome and rally to the next big success.

**Situation 9: Merger or Acquisition.** There are always two roles in both of these scenarios. The taker and the taken. The biggest difference between Merger or Acquisition is the level of power each entity has. In a merger, it is more equal, although usually there is a more dominant one. In an acquisition, there is a dominant and a submissive.

Either of these scenarios are complicated. It is change and transition personified. It is probably the most profound and tangible change situations that most leaders have experienced or can easily understand. It is ripe with uncertainty and ambiguity, but it is a classic change situation with epic opportunities for innovation.

The complexities of this situation include strategy, operations and infrastructure, resource consolidation, emotional volatility, and much more. Once all the paperwork, lawyers, and financiers are done, the hard work really begins.

*Optimal Response:* Regardless of which side you are on in the deal, you should handle this situation the same. You must set the tone for your team and lead. You should have a humble confidence. You should reassure, but make no promises because there are so many unknowns.

In particular, you should start with the empathy skills from the *Pleaser*, because no matter what, this will be stressful and scary. You must keep a pulse check of the feelings, thinking, and experiences of everyone involved — your team, the other team, your managers, other managers, your peers, and soon-to-be peers.

Next, you want to bring in your *Imperialist* metrics skills to compare data on both fronts and frame up the first pass of how to progress forward on the restructure. You also want the *Imperialist* to identify early key wins to calm the organization and build confidence in its new form and direction.

Finally, you want your *Explorer* to quickly merge the teams and set them in a productive, collaborative motion to define the best go-forward path by sharing best practices, pain points, and overcome cultural differences. You have an opportunity to make significant changes in mindset, process, and frameworks to discover and deliver innovation systemically with these newly united forces.

Inevitably you are going to have to cut people, transition systems, and integrate new products and solutions. You will need the Leadovator skills to help do this with strategic agility in mind. You will need to view all these actions with digital relevancy in mind.

- *Is this an opportunity to ditch legacy systems and operations?*
- *How can we best communicate, monitor, and manage leveraging digital platforms to connect beyond function or geography?*
- *How will we merge disparate data sets to understand opportunities and threats in this new structure?*
- *Who do we need to help do that now, and then who to manage and analyze in the future?*
- *How can we tackle the complex problems through design thinking or lean startup methodologies?*
- *How can we establish a new cultural norm of fail fast and move at Smart Speed?*
- *How can we clearly communicate our intentions consistently, and frequently reframe and update along the way?*

These are the opportunities a merger and acquisition can offer, but it will be messy, stressful, and complex. It will be a constant state of ambiguity and uncertainty. It will be a change on a magnitude that can make or break you if not handled with calm, confidence, and poise. Above all, it must be presented as a constant work in progress, an organic and evolving entity that is customer and market focused, and powered by brilliant, innovative employees.

**Situation 10: Market Transitions.** Market transitions are pretty self-explanatory — they are changes in markets, industries or economies. They are fueled by changes in technology, policy, demographics, and a litany of other factors. They are the ultimate opportunity for growth or decline depending on how an organization anticipates and responds.

These are the diamonds in the rough you absolutely want to capitalize on. And they aren't as black and white as in the past. Industries, business models, and customers are mixing and mingling like a frothy cocktail. It's hard to see where the lines are, if there are any lines at all. You have companies like Walgreens™ that went from retail pharmacy turned Minute Clinic™ providing flu shots, vaccines, and other professional medical services. You have Amazon™ that goes from online retailer to one of the largest hosting and storage companies in the world with AWS, Amazon Web Services™ while no one was watching. You have tech giant Google™ that transitioned beyond just a major Internet search engine to self-driving car creator, business applications developer, GPS system provider, and mobile operation system provider. The list goes on and on. These companies saw indicators of a major disruption and rallied resources to capture the opportunity. Companies that do this well are always described as innovative. They would absolutely be defined as the *Nimble Innovation Powerhouse* in our organizational assessment.

*Optimal Response:* This is your end game. This is the whole reason you are reading this book, you are pushing yourself beyond your norm, and you are going to push your team toward the innovative. This is why you need a league of INTRApreneurs at the ready to monitor, discover, and activate. This is why you are going through the painful transition. This is it. You want to be able to capture these market transitions at Smart Speed — Intelligent, Quick, Successful and Continuously.

Similar to the merger and acquisition scenario, this will take the whole suite of skills and attitudes to successfully capitalize on market transitions. It is not a lone venture. It will not only take these general skills and attitudes of one leader, but a community of leaders and employees with the same strategic agility mindset across function and ecosystem and the practice to deliver.

You must employ all of the archetypes, skills, and attitudes both traditional and modern if you are going to win.

You need to have the *Explorer*, who wallows in ambiguity, fully digitally fluent and at the ready, constantly looking for disrupting forces as they emerge. You need to have the *Pleaser* with the human-centered empathy keeping a pulse on the experiences of her/his customers, partners, and prospects, understanding pain points or gaps. You need the *Imperialist* with a power pack of modern analysis skills applied to business-as-usual KPIs to find blips that may be indicators.

You must have prepared your whole organization on new agile and iterative approaches to problem solving that includes customer and stakeholder validation and co-creation. Your *Explorer* leader will lead the way with outcome-based collaboration among the entire matrix of your ecosystem, leveraging modern problem solving frameworks to fail fast and learn faster. You need to tag in your *Pleaser* to build consensus of a direction when the fork in the road splits and rally everyone around a common direction. Then slide in the modern expansive view of resource management beyond the direct control with ninja recruiting and delegation skills of your *Imperialist* to activate and align for the quick win and the first mover's advantage in the market transition. You celebrate the victory, rest a bit to reenergize, and then it's go time again.

Tag in your *Explorer* again to begin the next phase of adaptability where this first win will lead when all information is not fully available. At the same time, you will be relying on your *Pleaser* delivering on the quick win promise with mad project management skills and managing by a predefined objective, with a strong sense of direction provided from your *Imperialist*. You celebrate the victory, rest a bit to reenergize, and then it's go time again.

Then repeat again and again with new market players, new rules and regulations, new partner dynamics, and your INTRApreneurial workforce flexing like the ebb and flow of the tide without resistance, and at Smart Speed.

This is what you have been training for, this is the Super Bowl or World Cup of business: capitalizing on market transitions at Smart Speed. This is the "why" of *The Innovation Revolution* and the knowledge and capacity to make the leap and transition is within your reach.

These situation overviews are extremely simplified to demonstrate the various strengths in each archetype and how they apply to common scenarios inside an organization. They were to acknowledge the complexities faced by leaders and to demonstrate how each leader type brings value. As you consider which skills you possess, notice the areas you are less comfortable with and strive to improve these skills or attitudes. You must also build capacity in the Leadovator skills list. It is the only combination that will help you usher innovation within at Smart Speed, cultivate and nurture INTRA-preneurship, and transform your organization systemically.

*How to develop complementary skills to deploy the best leader archetype combined with modern Leadovator for these frequently encountered situations?*

**3 Simple Starter Development Tasks:**

1. **Find peers** that are each of the leader archetypes and form a master-mind mentor group to learn and advise.
2. **Research or take classes** in the skills you need to develop to build confidence and capacity in your leadership performance.
3. **Be open** to different styles and approaches, as they can benefit across a variety of situations you will face in your career.

Here are some exercises to help you learn, apply and practice both Leadovator skills and the other top leader archetype aptitudes to lead *The Innovation Revolution* and usher innovation that impacts continuously:

**Digital Fluency.** Digital fluency refers to understanding how to harness the new digital dynamic where technology and systems are fundamentally changing the way we live, work, play, and learn. It's understanding how to assess and implement technology to become more efficient, flexible and innovative.

**3 Simple Starter Development Tasks:**

1. **Learn to code.** Take an online course, go to a code camp or a traditional lecture. More than likely, you will not be the one programming, but it is important you have a foundation of how the logic works and what it takes.
2. **Participate online.** Read blogs, comment, tweet, update your status, video, text or even Snapchat. You don't have to do these all the time, but it is important for you to have some experience in how these things work, including how information is shared and experienced in this new digital dynamic.
3. **Shadow an engineer or developer.** Whether it is hardware, software or operating systems, you need to understand how a technically-minded

practitioner thinks and works. Take them to lunch or breakfast, build a relationship to have a better understanding of the ecosystem and how it works and is evolving.

**Analysis.** This is not your mama's analysis skills of times past, but a far more complex skill to understand how to collect and unite data from various sources, aggregate and apply through technology, and then review and discover actionable intelligence and insights, at speed.

**3 Simple Starter Development Tasks:**

1. **Research big data trends and tools.** You need to have a baseline understanding of this industry because no matter what you do, it will affect you. The convergence of data and cracking the insights code are the future. There are plenty of free trials, demos, and white papers to get you up to speed quickly.

2. **Explore the data tools in your organization.** You need to understand how your company collects, stores, connects and analyzes that data so you can effectively have access and discern insights from it.

3. **Shadow a data scientist.** On your next project that requires some new data modeling, ask one of your analysts if you can sit in when they start framing the task. Ask questions of why and how. By understanding how data sets are created, you will know the best way to analyze them or increase your confidence on what insights you receive from them. Bring donuts or brownies to sweeten the deal.

**Problem Solving.** Combine your best logical and scientific problem analysis, framing, and concepting skills with disciplined practice of design thinking. You then discover the solution through making, applying human empathy of feeling, thinking, and experiencing — across the users and all stakeholders in the chain of delivery, through an iterative prototyping discipline: framing, discovery, reframing, testing, improving, and delivering. Boy, was that a mouthful. Regardless, it is the most effective way to solve real challenges with powerful talent at speed consistently.

**3 Simple Starter Development Tasks:**

1. **Research design thinking, lean startup methodologies, and agile development.** These are the three hottest techniques in today's hyper-connected and dynamic environment of today. Google the topics, learn the basics.

2. **Experience a workshop based on these new methodologies.** Go to one at your company or with your team or with complete strangers. You can find them in your community in the form of meetups, Startup Weekends, and hackathons. IDEO offers a free in-person design thinking class. You must experience it before you can wrap your head around it. Remember, most, even you, are afraid to go outside the lines because of the unknown, and mitigate that through the power of discovery and experience.

3. **Try some activities with your team.** The best path to success is getting the problem right, and you need new ways of delivering as the environment changes. Have someone facilitate a creativity session based on any of these methodologies. You have to experience it in your environment to understand the next steps to evolve to this nonlinear approach.

**Resource Management.** Today's modern resource management has more to do with the resources you indirectly influence and leverage vs. the ones you control, such as your operating budget or your direct employees. It's the ability to understand resources among your matrix of stakeholders — inside, outside, and around the organization and its partners and customers, and how they contribute to your solution or competitive advantage. It's understanding how to harness and direct without explicit control over those resources.

**3 Simple Starter Development Tasks:**

1. **Create a customer journey map to take inventory of your new indirect resources.** Map out the entire process of how an idea becomes a product or service in your organization. Map the entire process and touch points from development to sales to support. Draw it out on a whiteboard or long piece of paper, noting who is involved at each stage and what is done at each stage. This will give you a visual representation of all the resources available to you.

2. **Build relationships outside your team, department, and organization**. You can't influence anything without understanding and relationships. The modern resource management skills of today require relationships across the customer experience chain that you don't directly control. Start building the foundation now. Meet people in every function throughout the customer journey. Build relationships through breakfast, lunch, or after work drinks.

3. **Bring in outsiders to your brainstorming or work sessions.** You, your team, and organization must get used to co-creating outside of the walls of your office or company. To execute the learn, develop, test, and adapt model of today, you co-create with your customers and partners instead of hiding it all until the big, potentially irrelevant, reveal. It's scary letting outsiders in on the mess, but it is the only way to move quickly and influence all your resources to meet the needs of *The Innovation Revolution*.

**Clear Communication.** It's no longer giving commands, but framing and reframing challenges collectively with your team and others, among all the ambiguity. It's setting constraints with built-in flexibility. It's trading in the buzzword bingo for clarity and broader reach. It's asking questions instead of giving answers. It's collectively sharing insights together to get to the root cause. It's saying what you mean instead of relying on inference and assumption. It's adapting language and terms to increase the understanding across diverse stakeholder groups.

**3 Simple Starter Development Tasks:**

1. **Ask your team to playback and add.** If you want to understand if you are being clear and if your audience gets what you are saying, you have to ask. Tell your team you are trying to develop clarity in your communication and you need their help. After a planning session, ask your team to repeat back what you have said and invite them to add their own insights. This not only helps you understand if you are clear, but it also invites them into the process, which is far more collaborative and effective.

2. **Ditch the buzzwords.** Just stop using them if they aren't relevant. Get a buzzer and institute a buzz when someone uses a buzzword that isn't relevant similar to the game Taboo. It's a fun way to help simplify and clearly communicate for inclusivity and understanding.

3. **Cut it out.** Stop creating presentations containing 50-100 slides. Stop going over time allotted for a presentation or read out. Shrink meetings from one hour to 45 minutes. Less is more and it takes discipline and practice to select specifically what needs to be communicated to get to the next action. Use a visible timer when you have review meetings and set up a time boxed agenda. Communicate the time constraints beforehand and the method in which you will call time. I find calling time by everyone clapping at the buzzer is a community-driven way to

keep everyone on schedule. No one is the timer keeper or bad guy and it's all in service of the best use of time for the team and others.

As you are learning and practicing these skills, you will feel uncomfortable, but that means you are doing it right. Innovation is the antithesis of normal. Only by living at the edge of your comfort zone can real innovation emerge. Breathe, you got this!

# Chapter 12

# Dealing with the "F" Words – Fear, Focus, Frustration

*"Barriers to innovation are usually in the mind."*
*— Ratan Tata*

Promise of the Chapter:

- Discover signs and reactions of fear and methods to combat.
- Reveal focus as the biggest secret to innovation success.
- Learn how to A.C.E. frustration to persevere past setbacks on your Leadovator mission.

In order to have any chance to lead *The Innovation Revolution*, you must manage these top three "F" words:

## Managing Fear

The number one "F" word in innovation — is Fear. Fear is enemy number one. It is the Lord Voldemort of innovation or action. It is the single largest obstacle we all have to overcome. It can be fear of failure, fear of imperfection, or fear of uncertainty. Fear is natural. Anthropologically, fear is what kept early humans alive as they battled real threats from wild beasts. But, let's be honest, your career is NOT analogous to running from lions or bears. Sometimes it feels that dire, but it is NOT the same. So that very innate, natural emotion created to protect us, actually hinders our ability to progress forward into the unknown.

Flight or fight is real. Since our mind is prone to play tricks on us, I always suggest looking for physical warning signs. Your body doesn't lie, although we try to ignore its cues. Your physical manifestations may differ, but they are there. Tuning your awareness to physical cues will help you recognize when fear arises and then allow you to take action. Your ability to manage fear is the super power needed to carry out this *Innovation Revolution* in the enterprise.

**Six Physical Signs — the Billboard of Fear:**

1. Belly gurgle or a burning or twisting feeling in your gut.
2. Hot or cold face.
3. Forehead sweat.
4. Body fatigue.
5. Tear-jerk.
6. Breathlessness.

These physical signs are all on a long continuum. Some people have an extreme reaction while others mild. Unless you are a sociopath, you will have these physical reactions in some form.

Once you recognize these physical signs, you can now take action to mitigate the harm they cause you, your team and organization. I use the HERO formula.

HALT EVALUATE REFRESH ONWARD

Halt. Stop what you are doing.

Evaluate. Ask: *What are you doing? Why is it conjuring up this fear? What can you do to build more confidence in the situation to move forward?*

Refresh. Focus on the outcome and tweak your plan or actions accordingly to build strength to press on.

Onward. Lean forward into that fear by putting a new plan in place and letting go so you can move forward.

This formula isn't just for you as a Leadovator, but a tool you can share with your organization. It will help overcome the extreme pull of the status quo. It is essential to lead *The Innovation Revolution* and transform your organization to systemic innovation.

The size of the innovation threat of fear warrants a few more strategies to overcome. Here are 6 other fear-busting strategies you must incorporate to lead the *Innovation Revolution*:

**Discover the courage within and share it with others.** A wise friend and mentor always reminds me of an important fact when I face uncertainty and doubts. She says, "If it were easy to live bravely, everyone one would do it." That is wholeheartedly true. It's a quote I have on a wisdom pillow on my bed. It's the last thing I see at night and the first thing I see in the morning. I share this with you because it is the one thing that constantly inspires me to push forward. It reminds me that bravery is a choice, not fate. You have all the courage you need right now within yourself. You were born with it. Courage is something we never think about within ourselves, but sure notice in others. Courage is vital to lead *The Innovation Revolution* and evolve the enterprise to systemic innovation at Smart Speed.

## Six Strategies to Overcome Fear to Lead *The Innovation Revolution* Forward

1. **Start Small.** It sounds so simple, juvenile almost, but it is a classic that will build courage for the long haul. Evolution didn't happen in an instant and neither does innovation. People always underestimate what they can do in a moment, a month, or a year even, but over a lifetime you can accomplish greatness by ushering visionary progress one step at a time. It's not always sexy, but it's sound.

   Try a low-impact project and see what happens. If it works, then find ways to expand it. If it's a colossal failure, abandon it, learn, and try something else based on your insights. There's no better example of innovation on this front than Google. The search engine tweaked its algorithms early on to change the quality of search results. The idea was so successful with users that Google is now the most widely used search engine in the world, and the company's name has passed into our vernacular as a verb. But it also has had several colossal failures like Google Wave™ or Google Glass.™

   Small mitigates risk and exposure, which feeds the risk mitigation need. It's the way to try big ideas without the big bust.

   Encourage your team to always experiment with small scale pilots first and then go for the big launch. And a secret weapon to public experimentation is to use BETA in front of your solution. That sets expectations for the user so you can test without a big, fat embarrassment.

   The practice of experimentation is a key cultural norm needed to nurture INTRApreneurship to deliver systemic innovation within an organization. It helps everyone understand that both failure and success are knowledge and both are needed to deliver innovation. It will help everyone manage doubt and ensure a much better outcome through proof of concept, experience and knowledge. It thwarts naysayers and the legacy inertia plaguing the enterprise.

2. **Lean Forward into Fear.** All those big innovators, startup geniuses, and even empire CEOs splashed across famous magazines, TV shows, and the Internet, didn't make those big breakthroughs overnight. No, they had plenty of failures before then, but they kept trying. They overcame each obstacle by leaning forward into the fear.

Sometimes it takes grit and guts to make big things happen. And the answers are more often probable instead of perfect. Humans are irrational, so no matter how much testing and data you gather, you will never know exactly how it will all shake out. Embracing that uncertainty and leaning forward into the fear is the only way to demonstrate the courage you want your teams to emulate.

More times than not, that epic case you made up in your head will never become a reality. And since you are the leader, your team learns by example. If you want them to lean forward into the fear, then you must show them how. You have to be confident enough to show them you have doubts and fears too, and this is how you handle it. It is the only way people will acknowledge their own fear and face it head on. If they think you are fearless and they have doubts, it will only hinder their risk-taking actions, because they will equate this pseudo fearlessness as normal and question their decisions and selves even more. So stand straight, take a powerful breath, and lean forward. You got this!

3. **Power of the Pack.** It's crazy that we think we are all alone in this innovation quest. That the big decision to move forward is yours alone to make and yours alone to take the fall, if it fails. That is complete bullshit and is the very reason why your organization resists change and innovation. You are never alone. You have a team, you have peers, you have an organization, and outside of work, you have a support system of family and friends. All of those people make up your pack and are with you regardless how big or small the opportunities you take. They are there to cheer you on, sometimes find the story or data lever to seal the deal, and they are there when things fall apart.

Thinking only you can do this alone is insane,  untrue, and completely flawed. It takes the matrix of stakeholders to help make decisions and take actions to make it all work. It is a collective and collaborative effort from start to finish, regardless of the outcome. Know that, use that. Your team can help you, if you will only allow them. As a Leadovator you must have the confidence to share the load and the responsibility. Sharing the responsibility is the only way to democratize innovation inside an enterprise. If you are willing to share the glory and the downfall when it happens, you will create an ongoing flood of innovation. Remember, it's a whole lot easier to take down an individual than to take down a pack.

Nature has certainly proven the power of the pack. Look at wolves. They live, play, and hunt in packs. They know that if they all work together they will eat dinner, and if they don't, forces bigger than each individual could take each one out.

Forget this lone ranger mess and embrace the pack. Its power uplifts everyone.

At the same time, you must share this sentiment with your team: That they are not alone; That they have you, the team, the organization, and their support systems at home. You must emphatically preach this power of the pack, if you want your employees to embrace their inner INTRApreneur and take risks, adapt in the face of adversity, and question everything. Only through the confidence of you as a leader and the team to support you will these behaviors emerge and proliferate.

4. **Wander Down Memory Lane for a Boost.** You have made it this far, so you have some successes under your belt. *Am I right?* Ok, those successes not only serve as experience that help you make judgment calls on tasks large and small, but also help remind you of your success when tackling big risks in the past. It helps boost your confidence to take another and another.

Look back through your resume or LinkedIn profile when doubts creep in. It will remind you of the challenges you faced in your past and how you overcame them. It also might inspire the answer or the question you seek.

Sometimes others need to be reminded of your badass past too. You can use anecdotes of real situations that may be analogous to the challenge you are facing now. No one can resist a real-live-no-jive success story that you experienced and can bring to the table as an example. Memory Lane can be very powerful, and it will surely boost your confidence and courage.

You will find this stroll to be quite empowering, and, therefore you must share this same strategy with your team. When they hit a wall, either a process isn't working as expected, or they can't get the final buy-in or approval from a cross-functional leader, and they feel defeated and deflated, remind them of their past successes. Help them use that history to boost their strength to take the project to the last mile. Remind them why you hired them, point to successes you have seen while managing them. You must show them their own pattern of success and resilience so they can charge ahead.

5. **Trust Your Gut.** It's hard, venturing into the unknown, which is what innovation is. It's hard to trust your intuition when you may not have encountered anything like this project or product before. Compound that with the status quo, the legacy processes and past that are honestly no longer relevant. It's even harder since we now live in this world of infinite data. But you mustn't forget the human factor. All that data is always subject to interpretation and analysis. The numbers don't speak for themselves. And that is when your experience and your gut come into play. If there was a model or technology that accurately predicted the future, then we wouldn't need people or their gut, or any other company at all. Since humans are on the front and back end of all that is created, you being a human being more than gives you the knowledge and imagination to trust your instincts. Instincts of your customers will play into their decisions when the final judgment call for the buy comes in.

   Your gut has the understanding of emotions, irrational behavior, and experience. It shouldn't be your only source, but it should be at least one. Your gut can be the invisible force to overcome your doubts.

   Next you need to teach your team how to trust their gut. That is much harder to do, because you probably aren't as confident of their gut decision as your own. But over time, you can explore how they made certain decisions and get to know their gut and influence it with yours. It takes time, but building this ability will serve you when the answers can't be found anywhere else.

6. **Engage a Support System.** No, I am not exactly talking about group therapy here. I don't think they have an "innovators anonymous." Innovation and change can be a lonely pursuit, even if it takes legions of people to make it happen. The champion of the unknown is always a target. By definition, innovation is not normal and when things are different, people tend to turn away naturally. Haters and know-it-alls are going to come out of the shadows to try to strike you down. The intimidated will find every excuse to destroy progress because it questions everything. Because the battle is long and intense, it is essential you engage a support system to carry you when you are tired and beaten down.

*What kind of support system do you need?* You need one on both fronts: work and home. Work is such a big chunk of our lives and bleeds into our personal life so much that is it impossible to be an Leadovator without a dual support system.

At work, you need peers. They should be both inside and outside of your organization. The inside ones are important because they can help validate your thoughts and experiences within the context of the culture of the organization. They can also be the ones to partner on projects, influence, and remove barriers. You need to create an informal or formal group of Inside Leadovators — internal leaders of innovation — that meet for breakfast, lunch, or cocktails once a month to talk shop. They can become a Leadovators league to help rally and legitimize the pursuit of systemic innovation within the enterprise. It provides an experienced sounding board for all involved, allows for some much needed venting and validation, plus it helps the overall organization push boundaries and operationalize innovation.

Then you need peers on the outside. These are the Outside Leadovators — external leaders of innovation who have the same aspirations and obligation to lead the transformation. They come in different forms. Some may be in your industry; some may be in academia, government or nonprofits. These are leaders that deal with similar issues and have a different perspective that can only help inform and share your mission. It's hard to get this group of leaders together, so I would suggest a quarterly session with the intention to share one innovation win, one innovation struggle, and how to make this pursuit more commonplace. Keep the sharing to three minutes each. The rest of the group should cheer for the win, take notes, and see if it applies, and then dive into some advice for the struggle. Keep responses to three minutes as well. If people want to connect after and get more details, then they know who to follow-up with.

Next you must shore up your friends and family support system. These are the people you can let your hair down with. These are the folks that don't know you has a Leadovator or Innovation Champion, but by your given name, Bob or Linda. They know you as you. And no matter your track record at work, they support you. They also ground you in reality, outside your organization. They show you that there is more to life than your paycheck or your title. They are your cheerleaders, your coaches, and sometimes, your sanity. Don't think you can fight the big innovation fights without them. And to further prove my point, neurological research reveals that influence by your peers and people you hang around actually changes brain pathways, which means you are who you hang out with.[43]

Whether or not you have Schwarzenegger biceps, if you are pushing real innovative projects long enough, you will need a spot every once in a while. Don't forget to cultivate these relationships well before you need them, otherwise you might be left in a puddle. Your team needs the same support system to help them be brave; share this advice with them and hold them to it. It is critical for systemic innovation.

Fear-mitigation strategies down, now let's move to signs of fear within your team or peers. These are outward reactions that identify fear at work and impede innovation as a convention.

- Indecision and Inaction
- Excuses
- Obstruction

If you notice any of these activities within your team or from your peers, you should send up the warning *flag of fear* at work. In order to lead people over the fear bridge, it is critical you activate your empathy skills. Understanding what underlying motivators are at play can accelerate a solution.

Let's dive deeper into these fear-based reactions.

Indecision and inaction can leave an avalanche of stalled projects, missed deadlines, and sometimes missed market transitions in their wake. Not doing something can be just as damaging as doing the wrong thing.

Here is the thing about decisions within organizations — the power to make them is in the hands of a few. Since that is the case, indecision is a major contributor to the sloth's pace of the enterprise. You have to go through layer upon layer of people in the hierarchy to move forward.

*Just flatten, right?* Well, that just shifts the cause of this dysfunction from layers to lines. Lines of people or projects waiting for one decision maker.

---

[43] https://en.wikipedia.org/wiki/Neuroplasticity

In the last decade, organizations tried to streamline and began to flatten. It's true that small, nimble startups can pivot in an instant because they are smaller. *But is flattening really the solution?* Flattening organizations hasn't helped because it just means that certain leaders are left making exponentially more decisions and with the infinite information available. They become bottlenecks. This doesn't alleviate the problem and causes another one — burn out of the smart and capable.

Today you are left with two undesirable paths for decisions in the enterprise:

1. Go through a maze to get decisions made, or
2. Wait in line for them.

Either way, indecision is a barrier and a reaction to fear.

*What if there are more smart and capable people available to make decisions to relieve the business log jams?* Empowering those INTRApreneurs to make more decisions alleviates the lines by removing the layers. As a Leadovator, you must push down the decision-making, you must empower and enable more people to make systemic innovation in the enterprise a reality.

Control of decision making is eroding with the increased volume of decisions and the flattening of organizational structures. Fewer decisions are made, more log jams accumulate, and the enterprise is falling further and further behind. It's time to channel your inner Elsa from *Frozen* and "Let it go." Not every decision needs to have an advanced degree. If a sales representative got the wrong order, they should be empowered to fix it, right then and there.

Which leads us to this conclusion: it is not some arbitrary, research-based decision-making framework that is going to save your bacon. It is actually your relinquishing control. That is the number one thing you as a leader must do. If you truly want to work at Smart Speed and usher systemic innovation into the enterprise, if you truly want to nurture INTRApreneurship in your organization, if you want to lead your organization into *The Innovation Revolution*, then you must empower your people to make decisions.

In order to do that, you must be confident in how they will make decisions. You should also feel confident that they CAN and WILL make good decisions. If you are training them to be INTRApreneurs along the way, this should be much easier than relying on traditional frameworks or hierarchy. You must teach them a method to make smart, informed, and confident decisions, just like you would, and be clear on what decisions are theirs and what decisions may need consulting with others.

It's the one we use in the Smart Speed Method:

1. Define the decision.
2. Collect both quantitative and qualitative information.
3. Define the options and implications.
4. Validate assumptions.
5. Double check the alternatives.
6. Decide, take action.
7. Move on.

If you do get new information, then adjust along the way. Remember, there is no perfect information, because change seen or unseen is happening all the time.

Granted, not all decisions are created equal, and that is where your experience and leadership comes into play. You get to decide who does what. But don't rely on your old school habits or MBA knowledge you got a decade or two ago. Times have changed and so should you. You have to assess the impact, the expertise needed, and the authority and accountability you hand out.

The upside of this decision diffusion is more than just empowering your employees; it's more than just empowering you. It's about creating an organization that can move at Smart Speed and systemically deliver exponentially more value. It's also about competing head-to-head with nimble startups with more might than your giant peers and competitors. It's about providing more value for your matrixed stakeholders up, down, around, inside, and out. Stop the fear-based indecision and insanity and empower through simple, diffused decision-making. It's the only way forward.

Kick those excuses to the curb with an **Open Obstacle Policy**.

Excuses are a manifestation of fear and a symptom of doubt. There is a difference between an excuse and an obstacle. It is important you understand the distinction and institute a no excuse policy for yourself and your team. An excuse is a reason why something was not done. An obstacle is what is in the way of you getting it done. *See the subtle difference?*

The difference is not only in presentation, but in tone and in intention. An excuse implies that it is all in the past and can't be undone, and an obstacle is something that is in the present, still with an opportunity to overcome it.

In the Smart Speed Method, there is no room for excuses. There is a finite amount of time and a transparent guide. The clarity is what turns excuses into obstacles. Knowing how things will be judged and how success will be determined empowers teams to push beyond. It presents a litmus test of what needs to be solved. Clarity destroys ambiguity and naturally transforms excuses into obstacles in need of clearing.

When an excuse is presented, dissect the statement and ask:

- *What was the obstacle that lead to this outcome?*
- *Is this something that can be changed?*
- *What are one or two things we can do together to move this forward?*
- *Do we need to pivot and change direction?*

It offers you and your team a way around the obstacle and dissolves the excuse or negative behavior that prevents change or forward progress. Excuses perpetuate the status quo as acceptable. Obstacles present an opportunity for progress.

As a Leadovator, you need to walk in Monday morning or in your next team meeting, and send out your decree. You have a *No More Excuses Policy* now. Instead, you have an *Open Obstacle Policy*. If you have an obstacle that is preventing your forward progress, bring that to the table and we will all work out a strategy to remove it.

## Four Keys to Overcome Fear-based Obstruction Through Diplomacy

Obstruction comes in many forms; some blatant ("We've tried that way before,") to the list of reasons why something won't work, or sleazy political plays. Kick obstruction's ass by inviting others in and by building trust and diplomacy.

*Do you remember the popular song 'Da Dip ' that came out in the 1990s?* The lyrics of the refrain were: *"When I dip you dip we dip."* Well, that is diplomacy — a funky dance. It's the idea that everyone has to give a little to make things work. It means trusting each other and letting go to move forward. It is imperative to activate *The Innovation Revolution*.

1. **Be Humble.** Every time I hear this word, I can't help but hear Indiana Jones' whispering-turned-yelling voice from the movie *Indiana Jones and The Last Crusade* inside my head. *Do you remember the scene?* The Nazis found the final resting place of the Holy Grail, but couldn't get past all the traps. They shot Professor Henry Jones (Sean Connery's character) so his son Indiana Jones (Harrison Ford's character) was forced to face the traps. Jones had the clues his father found through his research that would help him overcome these challenges. The voice I hear is Connery saying over and over... *"only the penitent man shall pass, only the penitent, the penitent ..."* Then Jones yells, *"The penitent man is humble before God. The penitent man ... The penitent man is humble. Penitent man is humble ... kneels before God. Kneel!"* Then Jones kneels and rolls past the decapitating blades.

   I don't know why that scene stuck, but it serves as a mind trigger for me to be humble and work with grace and humility. It's a powerful tool for diplomacy. It endears others to be a part of your cause. It defuses defensiveness and obstruction dead in its tracks.

   As we have established, change and innovation are scary for everyone. That epic fear of failure is powerful. It is important for you to help others overcome that fear. The best way to do this is to present yourself as confident, yet humble. That tone and demeanor is an invitation for others to consider, and ultimately collaborate. You must have others join your movement, your revolution, for it to work. Buy-in is critical. So pop in that earworm of Indiana Jones to remind you the power of humility and its effectiveness in diplomacy. You will thank me for it.

2. **It Takes a Village.** Another classic I know, but it's worth a mention. Rolling on the heels of humility is the idea it takes lots of players at different

levels and influence to usher change and innovation routinely within an organization. From the employee who pitched, to the engineer who may have coded the solution, to the finance controller who allocated the budget on time, it takes them all. In addition, in a large organization, it takes a critical mass of buy-in and support to persuade top executives the risk is worth taking. It's far easier to say no to one person, one team or one department, but when other departments, leaders, and teams are on board, that is an army of change that is tough to defeat.

Diplomacy skills can help bring peer leaders and teams into the fold without the usual status quo objections. Finding common goals and challenges and co-creating a solution together is the best way to fast track buy-in and influence.

3. **Two Ears and One Mouth.** My teachers used to say, "You have two ears and one mouth, use them accordingly." I can hear their southern twang now. Regardless of how it is delivered, that powerful statement is one of the fundamentals of diplomacy. It is a life lesson that has served me. You must listen to understand before you start talking or proposing. And don't just reply with what you had planned. You must listen carefully so you can pick up on common cues or challenges so you can work together. It's not just about parroting, but trying to truly understand with empathy, so that you all can work with your limited, overextended resources to progress forward.

   As a Leadovator, you are setting the example for others. You are establishing trust and empathy in the hopes that others will do the same for you. You are building the foundation in order to help others overcome their fears and join you in the revolution toward systemic innovation that impacts routinely. In the frantic pace of today's business, we mustn't overlook the power of listening and understanding. It takes time, but nothing will progress without it.

4. **Reframe to Present a Common Ground and Language.** As you are listening, you should be taking notes physically or mentally to understand what you have in common. Most stakeholders share common challenges; they are just presented in a different way or with different language.

For example, if there is a delay in your production, one stakeholder may have a problem in ordering because there is no inventory, while another may have an issue because the delivery was late, while someone else may not be able to place their media advertisement because you can't deliver according to the offer. These are all different challenges caused by the same problem. If you listen and pick up on specific language in how each stakeholder presents their challenges, you will discover you all are suffering from the same problem in need of a solution. You can fast track buy-in and understanding by communicating in a common language, repeating their issues as part of the overall solution. In addition, you have discovered your common link, and you must use your best diplomacy skills to endear these stakeholders to join your cause, in this instance, fixing the production delay. This is an overly simplified example, but you can see what I mean.

Reframing your project or solution to incorporate needs or feedback from your stakeholders will instantly build support. Using their own language is the secret to fast tracking that buy-in. This is an essential tool for your teams to master in order to operationalize change and innovation.

Diplomacy can create a strong community to negate the fear-based obstruction to move the organization forward.

Now that you have enabling strategies to tackle the manifestations of fear through indecision, excuses and obstruction, you will need a quick-fire guide of the top seven triggers of fear which result in indecision, inaction, excuses, and obstruction, and how to help manage forward motion and progress:

## Top 7 Fear Triggers & Quick Fear-Managing Responses

| Fear Trigger | Response to Overcome |
| --- | --- |
| 1. Inexperience | Support is kryptonite to fear. Pair up an inexperienced employee with a more experienced person. Often it takes two to make a thing go right. |
| 2. Not enough information | Validation neutralizes fear immediately. Pose some unanswered questions to someone and suggest they do a bit more research – not just Googling, but validation with a stakeholder, partner or customer. It will beef up the solution and give the employee confidence to push ahead. |

| Fear Trigger | Response to Overcome |
|---|---|
| **3. Too much information** | Put your employee on an info diet. Give them permission to stop researching or evaluating and take what they have and commit to their best decision at that given time with that given information. Emphasize the importance of direction over destination. Remind them this decision is the beginning and that we will tweak along the way. |
| **4. PTSD from a previous failure** | Ask your employee of a time when they failed and what that felt like. Then ask them what they did after. Reassure them that failure is really just learning. Share your own failure to let them know that it is a part of the process. It also helps to share the batting averages of the Major League Baseball All Stars like Ted Williams, who still holds the record of .400 BA, which means he missed 6 out 10 times. |
| **5. Lacks confidence** | Your faith in an employee is the most powerful force against fear. Business is fierce, and sometimes an employee just needs someone to offer words of encouragement. Intentionally show them that you believe in them and off to the races they go. |
| **6. Restructure rumors or instability in the company** | Fear of losing one's job is a lethal force. Reorganization or restructure happens all the time in companies in both good times and bad. You know if the fog of hiring and firing has rolled in. It's important that you be candid, yet comforting during these times. Reinforce the needs of the business in terms of the project in play and reassure the employee that business is a team sport and we are all in the game. |
| **7. Unrelated personal disruption, circumstance or chaos** | No one escapes life problem-free. Personal issues and suffering are a part of life. The best solution to this is to ask if your employee is ok. Is there something other than work affecting them? Often a little acknowledgement goes a long way. Give them a little space and permission to take a break to confront what is going on outside of work and then tell them to refocus on the project the following day or week. The validation and pause will work wonders. |

There are always exceptions, but for the most part, these fear-busters will steer the ship on course. As a Leadovator, you are a lighthouse. Send the signal to build confidence, support, and validation, and watch the fear roll away.

**Managing Focus.** Focus is the single most prized possession in business today. With millions of distractions and expectations to face daily, this simple concept eludes us and erodes our progress. While the information era has supplied us with infinite information and access to it, it has also diluted our ability to focus and deliver.

I see this focus issue from startups to Fortune 100 companies, because you can do so many things today, i.e. blog, tweet, create videos, speak...and the list goes on and on. I find that people spend more time trying to do all the possible activities to promote themselves, their business or products instead of doing the most impactful activities well. Because there are infinite possibilities, the desire to do them all sabotages our efforts.

Researchers have proven having too many choices leads to anxiety, lack of confidence and dissatisfaction with choice. This concept was popularized by psychologist Barry Schwartz in his 2004 book, *The Paradox of Choice, Why More is Less.*[44]

To demonstrate the pitfalls of infinite opportunities and distraction, take the tale of two restaurant menus.

## In-N-Out Burger™ vs. Cheesecake Factory™

In-and-Out Burger is a family-owned, West Coast burger chain that focuses on simple quality burgers. The Cheesecake Factory is a national restaurant chain of American-style food with more than 33 featured cheesecakes available.

| In-N-Out Burger | The Cheesecake Factory |
|---|---|
| Only 5 listed choices: Hamburger, cheeseburger and double cheese burger, fries, and shakes. | There are more than 250 options on the menu, not including new items or specials. |
| Entire menu fits on one display panel in store | Entire menu is a book consisting of 20 pages, with additional featured special menu that changes frequently. |

---

[44] https://www.amazon.com/Paradox-Choice-Why-More-Less/dp/149151423X

| In-N-Out Burger | The Cheesecake Factory |
|---|---|
| Results: You only go to IN-and-Out to get a burger, fries and/or a shake. Since you only have a few select choices, you have less of an opportunity to feel dissatisfied. | Results: You have so many choices, you are far more likely to regret your selection because of so many options. |

This paradox of choice goes beyond lunch or dinner options; the same applies to business units. The allure of doing everything is seductive, but it is just a mirage. Everyone is constrained by time and resources. Although we wish we didn't have constraints and often the "canary in the coal mine" gets labeled as negative or pessimistic instead of a realist. Constraints are the only way to focus.

We can't ignore the pace of business and real forces of customers, the market and competitors, but we must be disciplined and discerning to invest in the relevant and the meaningful.

Zillions of studies have been done about prioritization and focus, lots of books have been published and bought, millions of dollars have been spent on coaches, and yet this simple task continues to escape us.

Focus is a like a muscle and the more we multitask and get distracted, the weaker it gets. The only way to turn those blurred lines into to crystal clear focus is to filter.

**Three Areas to Filter, to find your focus and ultimately extend that focus to your team. Only by focusing can you solve the challenges of today:**

1. **Physical environment.** There is nothing like the physical world and our environment to signal certain behaviors and actions. Take your home for example. There are certain things you do in each room or space you have. Consider what you do in your kitchen, bathroom, bedroom, or living room. They each have a different set up, different objects or appliances, which are purpose-built for the intended action. The same concept must be applied to your work space.

Set up spaces or locations for certain activities, like your office, which only has your computer or headphones to block distractions or a creative space with flipcharts, colorful Post-its and markers.

2. **Schedule.** *How many times have you said you are overcommitted? Does your online calendar look like Rainbow Bright vomited all over it with color-coded events that overlap?*

   If this is you, then it's time to evaluate. Don't let your calendar bully you.

   My colleague Marcey Rader (www.marceyrader.com), best-selling Amazon author, productivity and wellness coach, offers some simple yet powerful tips on wrangling your schedule.

   - ✓ **Pick three priorities for professional and personal accomplishments every week**. Before you log out or leave the office for the week, write these priorities on a whiteboard or large Post-it note. This will set you up for a restful weekend and focused week.

   - ✓ **Pick one meeting-free day a week to GSD, Get Shit Done.** Block your calendar and don't accept meetings for this day. You can always offer alternative times and dates.

   - ✓ **Create an absolute "No" list and set up responses so you won't give in during that moment of weakness**. Pick three things you will stop doing that don't serve you or your team. Create templates of email or verbal responses, so when these "opportunities" emerge, you are ready to assertively and politely decline to stay on task.

   While writing this book, I set up a "no list" to focus. I wouldn't take on new mentees or organize events until this project was complete.

   You must take control of your destiny. You are in control of your schedule. Remember that!

   Plus, you are a Leadovator, it is your responsibility to set the example for others to follow. If your team sees your calendar is overcommitted, then they will interpret that as normal and fall into the same habits. The best way to lead is by example.

3. **Mindfulness.** While on the surface this suggestion seems all hippy dippy, trendy bullshit, it actually works. Science has proven mindfulness is the key to focus and calm.[45]

---

[45] *https://hbr.org/2015/01/mindfulness-can-literally-change-your-brain*

I will borrow from one of the premiere global meditation teachers of our time, the *Sakyong Mipham Rinpoche* and the *Shambhala* approach to meditation.

## Eight Step Meditation Instruction

1. Set a timer for three to five minutes; that's all it takes.
2. Take the meditation pose — seated, spine straight, hands on thighs, looking ahead with a slight downward gaze.
3. Set an intention to begin, such as "I will work with my mind to develop focus."
4. Place your mind on your breath.
5. Breathe in and follow your breath as it enters your body from your mouth and nose through your chest.
6. Breathe out and follow your breath out as it leaves your body.
7. When a thought comes into your mind, gently acknowledge it and then lightly push it aside until you are finished your session.
8. Repeat until your timer sounds.

Notice how much calmer and focused you are. Notice how your thoughts have dissipated and only the ones that require attention bubble to the surface. Once we are in the moment, we can focus on making decisions that best serve our goals.

Here are some questions to ask yourself.

- *What is the real problem?*
- *What is within my control?*
- *What can I accomplish within a certain time frame, with the resources I have or can acquire?*
- *What is the roadmap of progress and key indicators of success?*
- *How can I be focused yet flexible?*

After you discover your path forward, hold the line.

There is one caveat to consider after making your decisions — the idea of flexibility and adaptability to new information. This is not an excuse to go back to your "wishy washy," unfocused ways, but a simple mindful reality we all face. Since change is constant, we must be constantly evolving, but directionally you must be consistent. Tactics and actions may change, but hold firm on the direction you have established.

I remember when John Kerry was running for president and the famous "flip flop" term was created. Flip flop is the concept that you hold one position on an issue and then change it later. The truth of the matter is that everything is fluid. Therefore flip-flopping is actually a normal intelligent reaction, not a weakness. Things change and you, your attitude, your focus should change too; however, you have to test a path or solution long enough to see if you should pivot or tweak. Change creates lots of noise and you have to be able to discern chatter from real intelligence. You have to stay focused and yet flexible, so you can help create these actions as cultural norms and de facto internal systems. It's the only way to mitigate the information crush and meet the complex demands of today. As a Leadovator, you must clear the way for the sustainable, repeatable, systemic innovation needed to compete now and in the future. You are the key to *The Innovation Revolution*.

**Managing Frustration.** Frustration is a part of everything we do. It materializes in both the expected and unexpected. From a project that doesn't result in what you anticipated or predicted, to the business-as-usual barriers and bureaucracy to progress. It's a massively draining force. It sucks the passion and soul out of you. It can leave you defeated and deplete — two states where innovation cannot emerge, much less flourish.

Managing frustration is all about acknowledging, experiencing, and overcoming through expectation adjustment or creative problem solving.

Before you do anything, you must first recognize you are feeling frustrated. I know none of us want to deal with feelings. But feelings and emotions are what makes us human. We can't think them away; we must acknowledge they are there. We must take an inventory of how they are affecting us physically and emotionally. Then we must wallow in it. Wallow in the fact that we are frustrated. Give yourself permission to just be frustrated. Set a time limit. Don't problem solve, just wallow. Experiencing those frustration emotions allows us to let them go. If we jump to problem solving too quickly, the solution will be subpar and loaded with flaws that may sabotage the whole thing. After a good wallow, you are ready for battle. You will be able to redirect that negative energy into a force to break barriers.

Let's attack each of the frustration-creators one at a time: Expected and Unexpected.

Expected frustration resulting from business-as-usual barriers to progress. It's predictable – another leader is jockeying for position, resources are misallocated, or the system of feedback and approvals is infinite, take your pick. These are normal obstacles facing any change or innovation. Throughout this book we have described various ways dysfunctional business-as-usual impedes progress.

By now you have realized that is based on two crippling beliefs:

1. The incessant need for perfection, and
2. The fear of the fallout without it.

These beliefs are grounded in fear and the only way to combat these is head on.

Combat these fear-based frustrations with the A.C.E. (Acknowledge, Check, Evolve) Formula to ground your reactions and regroup to persevere.

- **Acknowledge** that these beliefs are systematically woven into the fabric of your organization. This provides you with much-needed perspective and empathy of the situation. Clearly seeing how these beliefs affect hierarchy, decision-making, processes, and systems gives you a path to sanity.

- **Check** your expectations of scope and timelines. You can't take on an entire system on your own. There was only one David and Goliath. Time is a powerful force. Sometimes allowing your colleagues to sit with the proposal is the one thing needed to dissipate the fear. Patience is more than a virtue; it's a weapon.

- **Evolve** your plan. If you can't get the next big thing through the machine, then evolve your plan. Go black ops and execute a covert pilot to show success to remove that final barrier. Or take objections and weave them into the plan, offering a more collaborative solution, with built-in safety nets for the fearful. Or regroup and spend your energy on a different priority. You must evolve your game plan to either go over the boulder, drill through it, or dig under it. This is a fundamental practice you must master and share with your teams in order to make the leap to systemic innovation. The path forward is rarely straight.

Next let's tackle the unexpected that leads to frustration. This is the stuff you can't control. You have navigated the tide of systematic barriers like a champ and, now you face an uncertainty. First of all, if you are pushing the envelope, this is a sign you are headed in the right direction, maybe you just hit a blind curve. It doesn't mean it's the wrong road, just something that is unanticipated. This is normal. Sure it's frustrating, but normal. Every pioneer has faced the blind curve of innovation. Don't retreat. Share this powerful insight with your INTRApreneurs, millennials, and Gen Fluxers. Setting expectation that a setback is normal is a way to minimize the frustration when it inevitably arises from the unexpected.

Acknowledge you are frustrated and why. Take time to wallow in it. Then A.C.E. it.

- **Acknowledge** the unexpected happened and document exactly what happened. Ensure you aren't looking at a false positive or you aren't just experiencing an anomaly.

- **Check** your plan. Assess the situation like a scientist. What happened? Why? What does it mean? How can we use this knowledge to move forward? Adjust one variable at a time to identify the missing element or where things went off course.

- **Evolve** your plan based on your new insights. Don't forget sometimes evolving means abandoning an idea or project. It may be temporary or permanent, but it is always an option.

**ACKNOWLEDGE CHECK EVOLVE**

Now you know how to deal with the "F" words — fear, focus, and frustration — of innovation and action for yourself. You can use these same tactics to arm your team against these nasty, yet normal aspects of *The Innovation Revolution*. Managing these "F" words is the only way to shift you, your team, and your organization to the strategic agility mindset.

# Chapter 13

## Motivation Matters

*"Motivation will almost always beat mere talent."*
— *Norman Ralph Augustine*

Promise of the Chapter:

- Offer top motivators of successful entrepreneurs that work for INTRApreneurs.
- Discover why intrinsic motivators trump cash-based rewards in the pursuit of innovation.

Think of motivation as "the spoonful of sugar that helps the medicine go down," — Mary Poppins.

Medicine, in this case, is delivering innovation and pushing beyond our comfort zone or the usual. Most of us as adults or professionals have learned to solve the same types of problems every day. Think about it. If you are in marketing, you may have a different campaign or product to promote, but the motions are still basically the same. To be asked to do something completely different, be that a different job or function, or in this case deliver innovation, goes against every fiber of your comfortable being. In order to push beyond our normal or the expected, we need the proper motivation to try something different.

Motivation is tricky inside organizations. For decades, leaders have been using the good old fashion carrot and stick methods, which are external, offer monetary rewards, or some sort of punishment, to motivate. For certain things, these work great. Spiffs (sales bonuses) for sales teams work to drive more product penetration in a certain area. The promise of promotion pushes people to take on more projects, responsibility, or mentor in a way that isn't explicit in their job descriptions. Therefore, these external methods are usually used to push employees to do something they are semi-comfortable; it is refocusing the same motion completely within their skill and experience.

On the other hand, when driving employees to create the unexpected or differentiated like innovation, those external motivators don't work so well. In order to usher systemic innovation into the enterprise you must motivate those INTRApreneurs differently — you must motivate them like entrepreneurs. Entrepreneurs are intrinsically motivated by their passion and interest. This creates profound meaning in what they do, which provides self-motivation beyond the monetary. This same need to find meaning in work is shared and vocalized among the millennial and Gen Flux employees who are quickly taking over the workplace by volume. They are demanding that meaning and purpose go beyond being just a cog in a wheel and getting a paycheck. That is a double bonus for you: knowledge that purpose and meaning intrinsically motivate innovative thinking, combined with a growing number of employees who expect it. That combo will help you fast track the business-as-usual transformation to Smart Speed and systemic innovation.

**Innovation Motivation Insight 1: Meaning and Impact.** Create a sense of meaning and purpose around projects to tap into your employees' passions and interests.

Another factor that provides intrinsic motivation and drives entrepreneurs is a direct connection between impact from their work. They know that whatever hard work or discomfort they endure — be that late hours or rebounding after the fiftieth rejection — that is all in service of their company, their cause, and themselves. They don't have to sift through layers of a big organization or make indirect links of their work and its impact to customers or unknown shareholders. Entrepreneurs are in it — getting dirty, raising investment money, selling to customers, or connecting with partners — making a direct and tangible link to the work. Entrepreneurs have no one else to blame but themselves (and perhaps lady luck). Working for yourself is a powerful motivator, not only because your dinner and roof depend on it, but also because every effort you make or don't make will end up affecting you directly. Directly understanding the impact of your actions, motivates clearly. And that is often what is missing from larger organizations.

Employees need that same link to drive them beyond the expected, to take the risk, to push themselves, and probably more daunting, to stand against the status quo. The further your employee's role or function is away from the customer, the easier it is to forget that work matters. The easier it is to be disenchanted or disengaged. And it's not just the size of the goal or outcome, but the completion and the follow through. Seeing their idea or their team's collaborative idea go from concept to completion delivered to the marketplace makes the direct connection of real impact.

Here is an example of the power of immediate impact: when I worked for a TV station and created a topical commercial promoting the 6 pm newscast, I experienced the immediate impact of my day's work. I saw it air on TV. I rushed out to tell my parents and friends to watch channel 11 at a certain time to see what I did all day. Thousands saw my work, including me. I saw and felt my impact.

So often knowledge workers don't see tangible impact and that has led to demotivation and cynicism. Impact is an intrinsic motivator and is critically important to drive habitual internal innovation at Smart Speed.

As I run these INTRApreneur sessions in medium to large companies, the most common comment from the post-event survey is the excitement and joy that their efforts made an impact — to their team, their function, their company, and ultimately the customers they serve. I have never received a single survey that didn't highlight this as a key benefit to the sessions.

**Innovation Motivation Insight 2: Challenge.** Demonstrate the unsolved challenge of an employee's innovation efforts to customers, the marketplace, or industry, to provide another intrinsic motivator.

Since we are on a roll, comparing motivational pulls of entrepreneurs to INTRApreneurs, let's explore the irresistible pull of an extraordinary challenge. Maybe it's thrill seeking, maybe it's neurotic, or maybe it's just the natural human pull to improve or overcome, regardless, a challenge motivates. No matter what article you read or interview you see with an entrepreneur, they always talk about this obsession with challenging work. Whether it is a problem no one has cracked, or no one has even discovered, entrepreneurs live for the titillation of the extreme, the puzzling, and the unknown. Challenge seduces your employees in a similar way. Consider why people pursue Olympic dreams. The impossible, the record, the pursuit to be the best or the first.

Researchers, career advisors, employee engagement experts alike always suggest that leaders and companies must challenge their employees to prevent boredom. It is estimated that 17-30% of people quit or switch jobs because of boredom.[46] They actually quit. That is far from the vision of delivering innovation. It does prove what a powerful motivator challenging and interesting work provides.

Providing challenging work for your employees can be complicated when resources are short and leaders have to figure out how to continue to deliver the less sexy, routine tasks of daily operations. Balancing challenge and innovation with operations is not a new issue for leaders, but it shouldn't hold you back from using this potent motivator.

**Innovation Motivation Insight 3: Confidence and Outcome as Recognition.** Skip the superficial monetary rewards and provide the reward of recognition and belief in the capacity of your employees to deliver innovation and impact within your organization.

Entrepreneurs have very limited paths for recognition. It's not like they can give themselves an Employee of the Year award or a Best Salesperson trophy. Nonetheless, recognition is vitally important for their success and serves as a mighty motivator. Instead of traditional company recognition programs like you find in big business, entrepreneurs must seek recognition from different sources, such as their customers, investors, or the media. This recognition serves as validation of their value, efforts, and skills. Employees need that recognition too, not in the trophy sort of way, but in the confidence way — That you, their leader, believe they are worthy of this meaningful, impactful challenge; That the organization recognizes their competencies and values their effort and work.

When I run innovation sessions with teams from large companies who could afford big pay outs, the rewards are usually silly toys and made-up superlatives to recap our shared toil and triumph over the challenge. It represents our shared experiences and the fact that I and others noticed them. The ultimate reward isn't some American Express™ gift card or a bonus in their

---

[46] *https://www.shrm.org/resourcesandtools/hr-topics/employee-relations/pages/many-employees-plan-to-quit.aspx*

paycheck, but a big after party to celebrate the effort, the ingenuity, and the experience only we could understand. And ultimately, it is the reward of executing the plan that came out of that session. That is the reward for participants and certainly the reward for the leadership and the organization.

You don't need sexy gadget giveaways or a flurry of dolla' bills to recognize innovative efforts. But you do need to recognize employees for both their efforts and potential.

**Innovation Motivation Insight 4: Balance as a Strength.** Provide a meaningful challenge that is still within your employee's skill set that balances a sense of urgency, impact and room for creativity and innovation to motivate.

There is one overarching concept you must accept when understanding motivation for employees to drive creativity, innovation, and transform them into INTRApreneurs and that is the notion of *"Not too loose and not too tight."* This concept comes from a lot of meditation practitioners when they are teaching you how to meditate and it serves as an excellent reminder of balance. If you are a Type A personality and you go to a mediation workshop, this notion will drive you insane until you really understand it. You see, we want exact instructions so we can reproduce an outcome, but exact instructions don't apply exactly because people, situations, and organizations aren't exactly alike. Therefore you have to make some inferences and do some experimentation to find the right groove.

Embracing this notion of *"not too loose and not too tight"* is invaluable when dealing with motivation for employees. For example, you can use this notion when setting goals for an innovative project. You want to set clear, focused goals in order to share understanding of the need or expectations so your teams can deliver. But if you set them too loosely, you will find people come back with ineffective solutions or they will be so distracted by all the possibilities they may come back with nothing at all. If you set those goals too tight, you prevent any creative solutions. Therefore, you must have a goal that is specific, but offers some flexibility for your team to bring their unique perspective and, hopefully, a valuable unexpected innovative solution.

*How the hell do you do that?* (Well, that is what I said at my first meditation instruction, and of course the instructor's reply was, "you will know when you get there ..." I won't do that to you.) It takes experimentation to figure out that balance based on the tasks, the people, and the organization, but I find the S.M.A.R.T. (Specific, Measurable, Attainable, Realistic and Timely) goal setting framework helps, with some boundaries that aren't strangling. It gives some constraints that create a box to work within, but also allows for flexibility in creation.

For example, you may want to take your biggest key performance indicator (KPI) and throw out a stretch percentage — we want to grow sales by 20% this fiscal year; we want to improve patient satisfaction by 10% this year. Don't say how. Just throw it out there. A diverse group of people will produce a variety of ideas to meet that goal that you never thought of specifically. Then you must refine after each iteration of brainstorming, validation, and prototyping. This way you get more specific with new **shared** information and experience. This is exactly what the Smart Speed Method produces.

This concept must not only be applied to the beginning of an innovative or initiative exercise, but also must be applied to the evaluation of the project and the efforts of the team as well. Your evaluation can't be so strict that creativity isn't rewarded or encouraged, but is also can't allow slackers to get the same credit as the folks that pushed themselves and delivered.

Considering the notion *"not too loose and not too tight"* when creating judging criteria of a competitive innovation session or even when doing performance reviews so you offer enough flexibility to allow and invite creativity and innovation to enter the equation. This is the only way to evolve the risk averse enterprise to a place where innovation can flow like a river.

Motivation matters. You must learn how to leverage meaning, impact, challenge, balance, and recognition to drive the innovative behavior of your team. It may seem like a foreign approach, but that makes sense when you are pushing for a foreign outcome like innovation. You must balance and incorporate the discipline of *"not too loose and not too tight"* when setting goals and evaluation for these initiatives in order to allow for innovative solutions to emerge. When properly motivated, you will build a league of INTRApreneurs delivering consistent innovation at Smart Speed. This is the endgame of *The Innovation Revolution*.

# Chapter 14

## Activate your INTRApreneurs and Lead
## Your *Innovation Revolution*

*"What lies behind us and what lies before us are small matters
compared to what lies within us. And when we bring what is
**within us** out into the world, miracles happen."*

—*Ralph Waldo Emerson*

Promise of the Chapter:

- Guidelines for creating and maintaining TRUST.
- Steps to creating an infrastructure for success to activate, nurture, and grow your INTRApreneurs.
- Affirm how the Smart Speed Method has all the makings of a movement to operationalizing innovation in the enterprise.

In Part One of this book, you were given a profile of an INTRApreneur, an entrepreneur on the inside. All employees have the capacity to innovate. All employees have the capacity to become INTRApreneurs. The traits that make a great INTRApreneur can be taught, and the environment for them to grow and thrive can be built. It is up to you as a Leadovator to nurture this capacity and build this environment for their success, yours and the organization's. It is the only way you will succeed with your *Innovation Revolution*.

Let's start with how to leverage the INTRApreneurs on your path to systemic innovation at Smart Speed. These INTRApreneurs are the key element to deliver this transformation from spot innovation activities to operationalizing innovation in the enterprise. They are the ones who will lead the solutions from idea to implementation. Without them, your *Innovation Revolution* is doomed to fail.

*How do you harness the tenacity and brilliance of these INTRApreneurs to deliver systemic innovation at Smart Speed?*

Let's assume these INTRApreneurs have the nimble entrepreneurial spirit and the enterprise skills to deliver innovation in your organization. Let's say they fit the profile: An artisan of some type — sales rockstar, engineering master, marketing genius, or finance wizard, and a natural problem solver who understands your offerings, customers, and industry. And they understand the constraints and opportunities inside your organization.

And let's say they have the following abilities within them already and can:

- Analyze a situation to determine the challenge.
- Make decisions on imperfect information.
- Create a vision.
- Communicate with passion that vision to the right audience for buy-in, support, and resources.
- Adapt the plan based on feedback and testing.
- Deliver through determination and discipline.
- Persevere in the face of barriers.

*These are all proven traits that successful entrepreneurs have, by the way, the only difference is the platform.*

What is left to successfully deliver innovation inside continuously is where you come in as the Leadovator and includes the following:

- Serve as a trusted advisor and champion.
- Offer a framework or guiding principles to deliver.
- Resource ideas.
- Align a team to support.
- Remove obstacles.
- Nurture a supportive environment, community, and culture.

All of these elements are within your power as a Leadovator. You must create the right environment which is safe and supportive for the wild and creative to emerge. You must rally up, down, and around the ecosystem to support and deploy these projects. You must serve as a coach and advisor, connecting concepts to relevant broader corporate initiatives, connecting experts and influencers, connecting the team, securing cross functional resources and budget, to fuel the idea forward to develop, test, adjust, and scale. These are all elements within your capacity to manage and contribute. Think of yourself as the guiding hand that lifts when they need support, blocks the naysayers and the bullying status quo, and pushes each of them beyond their own doubts to deliver innovation that impacts. This is your fundamental obligation as a leader.

What you are really trying to build is an internal incubator-like environment where you have multiple teams within your organization rapidly building and delivering innovations at the same time, at various stages of development, regardless of formal reporting structure. Unlike external incubators that have different startups working on various products and services that don't necessarily relate to each other, your internal incubator is focused on providing value across the organization and channeling the full might of your resources as an enterprise. You are positioned as the facilitator and advisor, and the organization is the platform, resources, and deployment structure. Having small, nimble teams working on iterative outcomes mitigates the size issue that often slows everything down. It allows for autonomy, agility, and a tangible progress. Sure, the teams will have to weave in, out, and around the system at first, but they can do that with focus, purpose, and your support to connect, influence, and protect them from the business-as-usual bureaucracy that drains the spirit and energy needed to deliver big. This is the gnarly transition, the path of quick wins using different methods whose momentum will power through the resistance with undeniable results.

### How can you serve as trusted advisor and champion?

You must first build trust. You will never have risk-taking, forthcoming, open-minded employees if they don't trust you, INTRApreneur or not. Remember trust is earned over time and unfortunately, can be depleted with one bad move. You must be earnest and act with the utmost integrity.

### Seven ways to start your employee trust journey:

1. **Connect on a personal level.** The notion "it's business, not personal" is WRONG. We spend at least 30% of our life at work. It can't be this objective, emotionless thing. People naturally want to connect; it's fundamental to being human. The level of connection though is variable, but overall people trust someone who knows them, understands what

motivates them, challenges them, and excites them. And it's more than just the work and expertise thing; it's the fact that leaders earnestly want to know how their life is going inside the walls of the company, and outside. And never forget this connection-thing goes both ways. You can't expect people to let it all hang out if they don't know you, too. I'm not talking about reading each other's diary. There is a definite line, but for the most part, it is a two-way relationship where you both have an authentic concern for each other's well-being and success in life and work.

You want to know if they have hobbies, a family, pets, perhaps their favorite band, sports team, or food. You want to ask how their weekend or vacation went and wait for the answer. These are essential ways to build connection and trust.

2. **Be honest and transparent.** If you are straight with them, they will be straight with you. You have to demonstrate the behavior you expect from them. You may not always be able to reveal everything at a given time as a leader, but you must be forthcoming, clear, and constantly updating the team on the health and direction of the company. Lack of information from you or the organization creates mystery, which leads to rumors, mistrust, and fear.

   I once worked  for a mid-sized technology company where the senior vice president (SVP) and head of the department left on my second week, which left no leader for three months. The new SVP came in, never pulling the global team together even for a conference call or video conference to introduce himself, share his background, vision, or priorities, for more than five months. You can only imagine the conspiracy theories roaring about the company. I'm not sure if he ever did have that big meeting. I left in the heat of all the chatter. Not only does that misstep propagate rumors, fear, and mistrust, it also leads hot talent to leave too.

   Finally, never lie. Once an employee catches you in a false statement — little white one or a big whopper — you are toast. Yeah, these sound like common sense things, but it's worth a reminder.

3. **Don't micromanage or dictate.** INTRApreneurs are independent by nature and demand autonomy. Those millennials and Gen Fluxers you want to recruit and retain are too. They see their leader as their peer of sorts with more experience, knowledge or influence, nothing more.

They see you as equals. If you micromanage a project, presentation, or email, you are destroying your trust quotient. They insist you treat them like the professionals they are. This bodes well for you, since you got into this to lead, not babysit.

Also, watch out for the boss-card or the dictator vibe; this will certainly build a wall between you. If you set the wall up, INTRApreneurs will shore it up until they can make their move to a more open-minded, co-creating environment. Dictating comes with an air of superiority that doesn't jive in an environment where you want employees to take risk, work together, overcome fear of uncertainty, and push the envelope.

4. **Show competence.** If you can't do your job, then forget earning trust. There is no fake-it-til-you-make-it with this special breed of employees. INTRApreneurs are artisans and internal badasses and if they sniff you can't pull your weight, then kiss that trust ring and all the innovation glory with it, goodbye. There is no way you can recover if you can't deliver your part.

5. **Be respectful.** It seems like a no brainer, but respecting people is integral to building trust. They are human beings with a variety of skills, and they are an integral part of the organization. So often leaders take their employees for granted, saying stuff like, "You are lucky to have a job." That is not the case for INTRApreneurs or top talent, for that matter. They are the ones who can leap in a single bound right out from underneath you. You must treat them with respect and they will reciprocate.

6. **Admit mistakes, share credit.** There is nothing worse than a leader who blames when something bad happens, and then hoards the glory when something good happens. If you want your INTRApreneurs to share ideas, learn to see failure as information and deliver despite all the harsh negativity and legacy inertia they have to overcome, then always share the credit and admit your own mistakes. It is a sign of respect, transparency, and models behavior you are asking of them. Chug your own Champagne my friend; it's the only path to trust.

7. **Never play favorites.** Your parents should have taught you this one, but in case they didn't, or if you were an only child, favorites destroy team dynamics. If INTRApreneurs think you aren't treating everyone the same, they will hold back or worse, use their influencing power for evil. Watch how you hand out assignments or share information. If you always give it out to the same person first, you will stir up a frenzy. Also, don't talk

smack about anyone on the team to each other; they will assume you do the same to them.

Now you know how to earn and keep the trust of your INTRApreneurs, we will move on to the mechanics.

### How can you offer a framework or guiding principles to deliver?

We are all programmed for rules, guidelines, grading, and scoring from birth. Your mama tells you to not touch a hot stove, brush your teeth, and go to bed a certain time. Throughout your schooling, you are given instruction, tests, and grades. And if you played any sports or participated in any extra curricular activities, there were scores and judging. There are social rules of decorum and politeness. We are taught cultural behaviors or taboos. It's logical to think we need rules, guidelines, a framework or process to deliver ideas or innovation. And if you don't set out this process clearly, an INTRApreneur will make up their own rules whether you like it or not.

You need some sort of process or mechanics to be able to receive, select, and implement innovative ideas; otherwise you may fall into the favorite trap of being bombarded with stuff you can't make sense of or you might get nothing at all.

When you are in an organization, you must ensure this process is clear, fair, and available to everyone. This egalitarian approach is the only way that everyone will support the final, regardless of whose idea it is. It's a failsafe to prevent defections or anarchy.

In Part Two of this book, we offered the Smart Speed Method that presented an event-based model as an effective means to overcome many business-as-usual obstacles, such as lack of focus, miscommunication, delayed decision-making, and misalignment of resources and people of the enterprise. You can unleash the pent up demand from your employees to share their ideas and transform them into impact for the organization, something they are desperate to do. It creates a pseudo-entrepreneurial environment for inception and validation with the power of global scale and deployment to follow.

Since the model is based on employees, and has built-in constraints, it overcomes the challenges of the size of the enterprise. It gives a framework that everyone can use. Your INTRApreneurs will shine in that environment regardless if their idea is chosen or not. It is a freeing experience that unleashes the innovation from within.

It is a strict method with flexibility built-in, and it works. I highly recommend you begin with this method to fast track efforts and shock the legacy system into making fundamental behavior, attitude, and cultural shifts to jump start the transformation. It is a way to quickly show success, teach hands-on skills, and thwart the naysayers and status quo through measurable results. It allows all levels to walk outside the lines with guaranteed success. It can be done quarterly, semi-annually, annually, or it can be used for an emerging trend where you need to move fast to seize the opportunity ahead of the competition.

Most of the time, INTRApreneurs just don't know who to pitch what to and then how to take that supported idea into pilot, and then scale. There is no clear path, especially with the interconnected nature and geographically dispersed reality of organizations, markets, and customers. It is getting harder and harder to share ideas with the right people at the right time, in the right place, for traction. And often the random ideas leaders hear, are just that, random. They may be out of context, shared with the wrong person at the wrong time, or not clear, or poignant. And yes, sometimes they are bad. It isn't entirely the pitch person's fault. Many employees don't know how to pitch or to whom to pitch, or what is important to a leader or to the business.

On top of all those obstacles — which are preventable by the way — you have closed and control hierarchical cultures that only think executives or senior managers or people sitting at headquarters or outside consultants can have ideas that are worth pursuing. It's ironic that many of these organizations pay lip service to wanting to inspire a more entrepreneurial culture. They pay trainers to come in and teach some of the skills and attitudes above or they give interviews about how open-minded and bottoms-up they are, but their actions send up a big billboard in lights that says: **We Don't Want Your Ideas** or **You Really Don't Have Any**.

Ok, I am stepping off my soapbox now. Bottom line on this one, you have to set some guidelines so your INTRApreneurs can delight and deliver for you. And you must execute consistently. *Remember the trust thing?* Well, if you don't consistently deliver, you will erode that, and then your innovation engine will come to a grinding halt! You can take that one to the bank!

### How can you resource ideas with budget and other things?

*As a leader, you control the budget, right?* Well that is the obvious answer, but ideas that truly make an impact are cross functional. It would only stand to reason that influencing your peers to throw in some money or some people would benefit everyone.

Those are two no-brainers.

Next, you can set aside some innovation money like a grant and when you set the framework and guidelines, let them know that is your seed money offer. A minimum viable product or plan doesn't cost much to test. Unfortunately, that is where enterprise titan traditionalists lose their way, because when they were rising in the ranks, it took gazillions to do anything. *Remember the big D — Digitization trend that is pushing markets and movement at light speed?* That trend has its advantages in that ideas and models can be tested for a few hundred dollars. You must open your mind beyond your past experience to try something different. If you want INTRApreneurs or other employees to look at failure as learning then you need to do the same. In this game, everyone plays by the same rules. You are all in this together. Remember innovation with impact is a team sport. *What's the worst that can happen?* So what if you lose a couple of hundred bucks? I bet that was the bar tab at your last customer appointment.

> **NEWS FLASH:** *If you have corporate credit cards, I guarantee you that some of your INTRApreneurs are testing with all kinds of software-as-a-service models using their corporate card. (Now after reading this don't go all command and control and audit your team's credit card statements and stop that INTRApreneurial spirit in its tracks). I know. I certainly did this when I was a practicing intrapreneur. When I couldn't get the budget, I would use my card or go "tin cupping" for some stray budget dollars. And certainly not all my bets paid off, but in the end the big ones more than made up for my losses. Takeaway — have an innovation investment fund for your team. Better yet, reach out to your peers within your function or integral function and up the ante. Shared funds equal shared ownership.*

One last thought about budgeting and resources for innovation. You don't always have to spend cash. Sometimes you can use the people and systems you already have to test an innovative idea, especially internal processes. Don't stop innovation efforts because you are resource rich and cash poor. Be creative, just like you are asking your team to do for you.

### How can you align a team to support?

This one is your sweet spot. You aren't a leader by accident. You have learned how to lead a team. You have learned how to influence inside, outside, and around. The easy play here is to set the priority for a particular project and assign resources, but the Leadovator play is twofold:

1. You should be setting the tone and culture with your team ongoing on the merits of innovation and the fact that it takes a team to persevere and deliver.

2. You should let your team decide who wants in and what skills are needed to deliver. This self-selection allows people to rally around their passions or curiosities — intrinsic motivators — that will serve as a 10X boost in productivity and quality. If you are serving more as a coach than a boss, this will be a natural fit. If you are earning trust, not picking favorites, and rewarding the right behaviors, this will be a slam dunk.

However, if you have not created this peer-to-peer, egalitarian environment, you must clearly identify and articulate what skills or resources are needed to successfully test and deliver this project; then let your team members volunteer. It is a way you can corral and influence without dictating.

Now if you need skills or team members from other groups to be involved, this is also a twofold scenario:

1. Your INTRApreneurs have been cultivating relationships across the functional lines. It's just what they do. If that is the case, empower them to recruit cross-functional team members to the project. Assure your INTRApreneurs if they need your help, they can count on it. You may have to talk peer-to-peer with a recruit's manager to assure them this project won't dominate their operational work.

2. You may have to use your mad influencer skills to get some buy-in from other managers. You may have to pull out your diplomacy and put it to work, reframing the project as a win-win, and assuring the leader you will share the credit as a joint project and partnership.

### How do you remove roadblocks or obstacles?

This is when you have to bring the heavy. You have access, influence, and power to remove roadblocks for your team. That may be a call, text, or water-cooler chat with your peers or executives. Removing roadblocks comes in all different forms.

- It is giving the "go" to your finance controller to release some funds for experimentation.
- It is getting your team on a committee call or customer panel to present and get buy-in.
- It is leaning on the next level up to take a meeting or give a "go" to keep everything moving forward.
- It is negotiating with your team on a proof of concept instead of the whole vision.

The best way to remove barriers is to constantly build relationships and earn social capital. These allow you to lean on them when the time comes. You may have to do favors or share resources when you aren't 100% on board for the return later. This is making that key introduction as a favor or even taking one for the team by going to the meeting in Alaska instead of Bermuda. If you are always giving, you are always building that capital needed to remove roadblocks.

### How can you nurture a supportive environment, community and ecosystem?

It has been proven in the entrepreneurial world that success in innovation and impact comes from creating the right environment, community, and ecosystem. Success for these entrepreneurial individuals and teams is largely dependent on reducing barriers, supportive infrastructures, policies, cultures, and diversity. It is also proven that entrepreneurs themselves must help build these ecosystems by inspiring others and communicating gaps and needs to leaders, lawmakers, educators, and community leaders.[47] The same principles outside can be applied inside to create a supportive ecosystem for INTRApreneurs within organizations. The biggest difference inside vs. outside is that the ecosystem is relatively small and identifiable. There are available organization charts and online directories. In theory, employees can contact anyone up and down the stack. The power, influence, policy-making, educating, and financing leaders are identifiable, but

---

[47] http://www.cipe.org/creating-environment-entrepreneurial-success

in practice, there is a lot of nuance. Titles don't always convey the truly powerful or, more importantly, the open-minded. This is where your role as a Leadovator becomes critical and impactful. You may need to grease the skids and influence behind the scenes to get a meeting or support. You have political knowledge that your employees don't -- use it.

- *What does this all mean? How does this affect you?*
- *What are you supposed to do to create this ideal environment, culture and ecosystem?*

1. **Lead by example for your team and beyond.** You have control over your team, its culture, and day-to-day operations. You have some level of power to set the example for others to follow. Set up a safe environment built on trust and support. Encourage your team to try new things and to learn from everything — success and failure. Use your influence for good by offering them exposure, funding, and counsel. Teach them how to communicate, modify with feedback, without being defensive and execute, execute, execute. Share your people with others when the right opportunity presents itself. Expose them to new ways of doing things with guests from other departments, partners, customers, and even other industries. Fight for them when the going gets tough. Protect them from over extension and burn out. Treat them with respect and honor always. Support smart sound projects, don't placate. Push them beyond their own beliefs and reassure them that you've got their back.

   Set the example for your peers across functions by delivering innovation large and small. Often peers may sling a classic excuse like this one: "I'm all for innovation, but most employee ideas aren't big enough to be considered innovation." That is someone who has a white-knuckle grip on the status quo disguised as a supporter to the internal innovation cause. Go head-to-head, and proclaim that statement is just crap. Innovation is change that matters, and if someone suggests something internal or otherwise that makes their work just a little easier, that **IS** innovation.

   Everyone needs practice at innovation, especially on a small scale to prep for the big ones. *Why do you think major league baseball teams have farm teams?* It's so those in the minors can practice for the big leagues. The same applies here. Your teams must practice innovating so it becomes second nature. It allows the innovators and the whole organization to practice. The more your organization becomes comfortable with change, the more change you can make, systemically and at speed, which is your ultimate responsibility.

Endear others to support projects and become a part of the movement. Support them since they are transitioning too. You will need to decide if you need to take a tough love approach or a more nurturing one, but don't let the innovation-crushing attitude propagate. If that kind of negativity builds strength, it will be impossible to lead *The Innovation Revolution*.

Your actions will send signals to your team and others you interact with throughout the organization. As a Leadovator, you are the proof of concept that respect, support, and coaching lead to successful innovation execution, not empty buzzwords or flash in the pan whatever. It takes old fashioned hard work and perseverance to make it all happen; there is no getting out of that.

2. **Be the connector.** Entrepreneurs are only successful if they have connections with influencers and investors, and the same applies to INTRApreneurs. You can connect INTRApreneurs with customers, partners, and internal stakeholders who are so essential to the validation and execution process of delivering relevant innovation that impacts.

   You can't have community without connection. And community building and nurturing is one of the new tenets of leadership. Remember, the matrix of stakeholders, inside, outside and around, even. You must be a builder. Networks of people are making things happen, not some singular silo in a mad scientist lab. It is diverse experiences and perspectives combined with a shared interest or mission that conjure new thinking, not the same old team hashing the same old solutions.

   This means you must be confident in yourself and your relationship with your team and other stakeholders. So often leaders get protective and become talent hoarders. Resist the urge and shut those doubts down upon entry. You need to introduce INTRApreneurs to subject matter experts inside and out. You need to help identify who has budget and how to influence that cash flow to your innovation project. Connections only strengthen your outcomes.

   Connection and community are the only way innovation is discovered and delivered.

3. **Listen with an open mind.** You must be able to listen with an open mind. You have to be able to block out the noise of a less-than-perfect idea

pitch or plan from experienced or inexperienced INTRApreneurs and employees. You must have the vision of an innovator to see beyond the literal and discover the potential that is embedded within a concept.

If you want others to listen with an open mind, you must show them how. You need to demonstrate what it is like to have an open mind. *What do you look for in a viable idea? How do you know who to pitch to? How to customize your idea pitch to your audience? How to get from idea to action?* All these insights come from listening with an open mind and then sharing those secrets with your employees.

If you want better ideas, you have to teach your people to listen to others and assess with certain criteria around: opportunity, match to the company's competencies or solution set, and execution viability. They in turn can support others through empathy and logical assessment. Open mindedness only comes when people are open to everything and know how to listen with an opportunity mindset.

4. **Encourage INTRApreneurs throughout the organization to speak up, connect and strive.** This is where you must empower your INTRApreneurs to speak out honestly on what they need, what is missing no matter how harsh or bold or ugly it is. It is the only way things can be addressed. You must encourage like-minded people to meet and share and encourage others to be a part of this essential group. It takes a groundswell of support to fight the status quo and legacy inertia. Everyone hates change; sometimes people that thrive on it do too. It is critical that these INTRApreneurs share actionable things that can help them push forward from an institutional and cultural perspective. They will only do that if the reward is worth it and there is a champion who will support and protect them as they fight the power.

When entrepreneurs in a local community work with government, educators, and business leaders to identify their needs and support, the entire community thrives. Entrepreneurs don't just help with economic development, but infuse this sense of promise and vitality that boosts the whole community. This is a classic example of President John F Kennedy's famous phrase, "a rising tide lifts all boats." The exact same logic applies to the INTRApreneur ecosystem inside your organization. When they thrive, everyone experiences an uplift.

5. **Be Brave — STOP the silly busywork, ditch the buzzwords.** The culture, the norm, the rules in any organization drive behavior within your

organization. As we discovered in Part Two, there is a lot of smoke and mirrors in larger organizations that are driven ultimately by fear of failure and manifest in superficial ways like meeting marathons, revision mania, and puff words.

Courage is definitely a theme in this book, but it must be. You must be brave to push against the rip current of business-as-usual. You must jump to soar. You must take a leap of faith for yourself, your INTRApreneurs, and your organization. You can't just exist. You can't just sit on the sidelines. You must push forward. You have a gift. You have a responsibility. You must help others find their gifts and fulfill their destinies to change the world.

It all starts with stopping. Every time you participate in any of those underbelly practices or buzzword bingo, you are contributing to the flawed system. The system will never change if leaders don't stop the superficial mess. If for nothing else but gaining some productivity and valuable resource time back, stop the madness.

Set up rules about meetings and email communication. It's pretty simple to require an agenda and needed outcome for every invite. Give people permission to decline if those elements aren't present. Have people talk to each other if an email chain volleys more than two times. These are all simple changes that build relationships and trust. This creates a safe environment for creativity and innovation to thrive.

Stop the lines or layers of approvals. Rally your peers to do the same. It takes a few small steps virally activated to *right* the ship. Enable and empower more people to make decisions and take action. You can be the change. You can stop the silliness and empower yourself, your team, and your organization. You are a Leadovator. YOU can do it.

All this sounds like a lot, but remember … start small. Start with introducing rules of engagements within your team, then branch out from there.

6. **Believe.** You must believe because the path to success is never straight. You have experience and poise. You must believe passionately. You have to believe when your INTRApreneurs lose faith in the fight. You have to believe because so many others don't. You have to believe because that is the very foundation of support that activates a community.

7. **Start a Movement.** Doing this as a one-time thing, just won't make a movement happen. It will be another singular innovation activity. Doing

any of the above in this book once doesn't make a trend and won't change anything. It will just be another blip on the screen and no one will notice. With a 24-hour news cycle and constant distractions, it is harder now than ever to stick to something. But you must fight the urge to be a one-hit wonder.

*What is a movement?* A movement is a group of people working together to advance their shared experience, purpose, and mission. The most important of all the words in that definition is the word **shared**. You must articulate the shared purpose of operationalizing innovation in the enterprise.

This purpose must be bigger than the individuals within it. It must be so great that it can overcome the greatest of adversaries — the archaic, dysfunctional business-as-usual system of today. This shared purpose must inspire. It must ignite the passions of the followers to activate. It must suspend individual or group identity just enough to unite behind a common cause, which will transform the world as we know it.

Your shared mission is to skip the slow corporate dance and perpetually deliver employee-driven innovation that impacts — the business, organization, customers, and beyond. It alleviates the shared pain of buzzword bingo, laborious bureaucracy, and disengaged employees. It inspires creativity, discovery, and transformation. It empowers and elevates. No more titles, no more hierarchy, no more levels or layers. It's accessibility regardless of experience or status, which is the opposite of how organizations run today. It's sharing power, responsibilities, success, and failure. It infuses the nimble entrepreneurial spirit and delivers at enterprise scale.

Often overlooked, setting expectations for yourself and others is critical. Innovation is hard. Transformation is hard. Fighting all the haters and naysayers is hard. No mission worth doing is easy. Setting the proper expectations can help sustain the movement. Missed expectations can erode miles of progress. It's our brain — it actually works against us. If we get what we expected, we will get a hit of dopamine; if we don't, the brain amplifies the negative sending a danger signal.[48] Innovation is the unexpected, but if others learn that innovation is the expectation, we can leverage the brain to support the mission and further the movement.

---

[48] *https://www.psychologytoday.com/blog/your-brain-work/200911/not-so-great-expectations*

One leader doesn't make a movement. You must have followers to make a movement. It starts with the one and then another, another and another. With each additional follower, you begin to build a coalition, a community. You must nurture each one. Share a sense of belonging. You must be grateful and humble. You must constantly remind them of the mission, validate their pain points, perspectives, and passion, and reinforce this work matters. You must nurture each one because they were brave enough to try, to do. It takes a supportive and caring ecosystem to create and sustain a movement. Without the care and feeding of your followers, the status quo and the resistance will win as it has for so long.

You have to make all these things routine to make it stick and create a movement. You must be vigilant. You must repeat over and over until it becomes a habit. You must schedule your Smart Speed innovation events, integrate the practices into monthly staff meetings for small everyday innovations. Expect projects to start, intersect, decouple, and launch in a tangled mess. You must constantly practice innovation at every turn and every level. You must define what that means, not just a phrase on your badge or corporate slideware.

All of these things are intrinsic to the Smart Speed Method.

This book outlines and gives you:

*Your mission.*
*Specific actionable steps to start, build, and sustain.*
*A tangible path to activating your internal innovation engine powered by your talented INTRApreneurs.*
*A process to skip the slow corporate dance and turn ideas into action that impacts continuously.*
*A bridge from the expected to the unexpected. All you have to do is cross over.*

*The Innovation Revolution* is the movement that transforms the way inside innovation is discovered and delivered. It is bigger than you, your team, your organization — it's the next business revolution and a new era of leadership and management. And you are the chosen one to lead it forward. Get to it.

# Part 3

# Complete: You are Ready to Lead
## *The Innovation Revolution*

It's on like Donkey Kong. You have made it through. But this is not the end, it's the beginning. It's the beginning of a new era of business, management, in innovation and in life. It's the beginning of a new league of Leadovators infiltrating the business-as-usual scene armed with empathy, confidence, and strategic

> "It's on like Donkey Kong."

agility with the super power to flex. You are ready to bravely face the uncertain and ambiguous in service of progress.

Throughout this book you have been given:

- Trends driving disruption in business-as-usual.
- Assessments for yourself, your employees, and your organization.
- Narrative stories with warnings and questions.
- Proof points, statistics, and data to quantify.
- A mindset and a method to transition from the legacy to the legendary and fulfill those innovation promises.
- Exercises to stretch yourself, develop your employee INTRApreneurs, and transform your organization.

It's up to you now to save the enterprise, by taking your Leadovator responsibility and drive *The Innovation Revolution* to deliver systemic innovation, powered by a matrix of talented people to change the world. Now, go get 'em!

# About the Author

I have always been blessed (and sometimes cursed) by the need to go my own way. As a child, I didn't just color outside the lines; I used every crayon in the box to do it.

Fast forward to adulthood where I found great success in the corporate world. A few billion-dollar examples:

- Pioneered one of the first social media strategic plans for Cisco Systems — including a monthly online video program viewed by 120,000 customers within the first year, later garnering more than $1 billion in sales pipeline
- Launched a comprehensive marketing initiative for NC State University — which led to its first $1 billion fund-raising campaign
- Co-led the effort to raise $3.1 billion for North Carolina public universities and community colleges — the largest higher education bond referendum campaign in US history.

As challenging and lucrative as these jobs were, they all left me wanting, after a time.

Too many lines—not enough crayons.

In 2011, I left my corporate 9-5 and immersed myself in the start-up business culture — first volunteering with Startup Weekend on a national, then international level, before developing the Smart Speed Method and founding my innovation company, *48 innovate*.

My two companies, Ester Mae Marketing and 48 *Innovate*, grossed over a million dollars in two years.

*The Innovation Revolution* is my first book, and I'll admit there were times when I wondered what I had gotten myself into, but I do believe with all my heart and head that it's time for big-business-as-usual to change.

So I persevered.

I hope this book will inspire all the brilliant leaders to stand up against the outdated and dysfunctional systems that impede progress. It is time to stop being "ok" with bad business behavior and dismissive experiences. I want to inspire and empower leaders and followers alike to take a different path, a path that allows everyone to experience success while walking outside the lines, a path that leads to *The Innovation Revolution*.

*K. Melissa Kennedy*

# Acknowledgements

First, mentors matter. Thanks to my mentor and longtime friend, Christine Ramsey for inspiring me to quit my corporate job and do something different with my life. She has always supported my nonconventional and brave choices. Her quote: "If it were easy to live bravely everyone would do it," has been my mantra throughout my journey and I share it with all of you.

To write a book is a brave undertaking. The very phrase "I'm writing a book" is heavy with expectation. There were times when I didn't think I could deliver, and without so many, I may not have. Now we all know I did, and for that, I must thank those who helped make it possible:

Annette Blum has been my champion inside and out of organizations. She has always hired me when I needed it, and courageously explored new ways of doing everything with faith in my ability. She is a brilliant, progressive leader and a dear friend, whose comments shaped me and this compelling book.

Thanks, Frank Pollock, for enduring my constant resistance to writing this book, starting our Innovators Meetup, and many other ventures. Your faith, confidence, and perseverance made all the difference.

David Rose deserves more credit than I can put into words for my success and this book. He was always willing to accept alternative work arrangements, challenge me in radical intellectual debate, and continually push me beyond my own beliefs.

Then there is the balance to all the Type A helpers, Dr. Paula Berardinelli, whose empathy and compassion allowed me to find my powerful voice within and my life's purpose — with grace and gratitude, I salute you.

My uber thanks to Ann Ward, who was my invisible sounding board to concepts, puns, and anecdotes. Her creativity and like-mindedness helped me stay true to my uniqueness.

My devoted, loyal, empowering friends,  Lauren, Chuck, Jodi, Connie, Kendyle, Georgeanna, Becky, Barbara, Ashlyn, Amy, Pattie, Ben, Ginny, Joye, Rebecca, Susannah, Spif, Camren, Wendy, Smitty, Claire, Tracy, Susie, Kevin, and so many others that sent a supporting text at the right moment or forced me to have fun when I was blinded by deadlines and doubt—Thank you all.

Thanks to my family for supporting this rebel with love and faith.

Thanks to my team – Diana, Leslie, Junnaliza, Amy, Marcey, Scott, Ellen, Magdalena, and so many others. We did it!

Writing a book is the hardest thing I have ever done. It requires dedication, focus, introspection, faith, passion, endurance, a little crazy, intellect, courage, and love. I admire those who have written before and those who have yet written. Cheers! I am honored to be in the club.

# Leadovator Action Index

Below is an instant reference guide to the action steps to help you transform into a Leadovator and successfully lead *The Innovation Revolution*.

# Glossary of Terms

Listed in sequential order as they appear in this book.

| | |
|---|---|
| Leadovator | 21st century leader poised to deliver consistent innovative results at speed by empowering others inside the enterprise to usher in *The Innovation Revolution*. |
| INTRApreneur | Entrepreneur on the inside, or Gifford Pinchot defined an INTRApreneur as a person in a large corporation empowered to create new products without being constrained by standard procedures. |
| Generation Flux | Also referenced as Gen Fluxers. A psychographic designation of brilliant multi-generational employees who thrive in reinvention and disruption and expect respect, autonomy, and appreciation in their work. This term was originally coined by Robert Safian in Fast Company article: https://www.fastcompany.com/section/generation-flux |
| Big Quit Movement | A mind-blowing employee exit from employment despite an uncertain economic future. |
| Legacy Inertia | The concept that organizations stick with the same process, tech, people, and solutions because they know the outcome, business-as-usual. Thanks to PRSONAS CEO David Rose for this brilliant term! |
| Blame Cord | The option to blame an outside party for failure; A hidden feature of hiring old guard strategy firms. |
| Appegeddon | The concept that a software application can solve everything. |
| Rip & Duplicate or R&D | The concept where you find a best practice from another industry or practice and adopt it for your organization. |

| Pleaser Leadership Archetype | A leadership profile that embraces empathy, seeks approval of others, finds it difficult to express true feelings and thoughts, fears rejection. Represented in the book as Bobby Ewing. |
|---|---|
| Explorer Leadership Archetype | A leadership profile that embraces uncertainty, acts selflessly to do the right thing, engages in dialogue not debates. Represented in the book as Peggy Olson. |
| Imperialist Leadership Archetype | A leadership profile that delivers no matter what, uses I/Me/My frequently, dislikes bad news, strives to be in charge. Represented in the book as Francis Underwood. |
| C.U.R.E. | A tool to assist a leader to recognize default actions and transition to new ones. C is for Curiosity; U is for Understanding; R is for Recognizing; E is for Effort. |
| Nimble Innovation Powerhouse | The organizational type that has innovation and wants to continue to grow it. |
| Innovation Comeback Kid | The organizational type that once was innovative and lost it, but can still make a comeback. |
| Hierarchical Innovation Crusher | The organizational type that got lucky, but can't innovate or survive in the future. |
| Over-rotate | The concept when someone rotates too far on a decision or direction which hinders or negatively affects the outcome or goal. |
| Smurfizing | The concept of overusing a buzzword to build some sort of cache or credit when it isn't relevant. The reference comes from the popular cartoon, "The Smurfs," where Brainy Smurf explains how the Smurf language works, which is to replace any noun, verb, adjective or adverb with "smurf." |
| Chart junk | Unnecessary visuals or verbiage on presentation slides. |
| Solutionator | Someone who is certified to facilitate the Smart Speed method and serves as a hybrid facilitator and consultant. |

| Avalanching | The process of piling on all the negative or unexpected things happening in our lives both at work and play until a crash. |
|---|---|
| H.E.R.O. | A formula to help you recognize and overcome fear in the pursuit of change and innovation. H is for Halt; E is for Evaluate; R is for Refresh; O is for Onward. |
| Excuse | The reason why a task or project was not complete. |
| Obstacle | What is in the way of completing a task or progressing a project forward. |
| Open Obstacle Policy | An office policy that prohibits any excuses, yet instead asks team members to bring forward people, policies, or other items, called obstacles, in the way of project progress. |
| GSD | Stands for Get Shit Done |
| Absolute No List | A list of actions you stop doing that don't serve you or your team. |
| A.C.E. | A formula for leaders and team members alike used to ground reactions and regroup to persevere. A is for Acknowledge; C is for Check; E is for Evolve |

## A Special Bonus from Melissa

With your copy of *The Innovation Revolution*, you are ready to inject the nimble, entrepreneurial spirit **back** into the enterprise with the genius hiding in plain sight.

Armed with proof of the complexity and intensity you face day-to-day, you know where to start, and where you must go. You are empowered to stand up and say NO to all that is impeding your path forward. AND, you are loaded with tools to make it happen.

For your courage to lead against business-as-usual, you deserve a little something special.

Here is my bonus gift for you:

- Discover your own hidden genius and ensure success with the digital workbook, **Activate Your Hidden Genius: 7 Surefire Actions to Ignite *The Innovation Revolution***
- Explore walking outside the lines and help make it stick with **The Weekly Zing**, an annual email subscription of weekly mini innovation exercises
- Take a simple **Three Little Orgs Innovation Assessment** to reveal your organization's innovation status and inform your next move

Go to http://innovationrevolutionbook.com/signup to access your bonus material.

Enjoy the ride in the driver's seat for your high speed, high impact journey to save the enterprise.

*It's on like Donkey Kong!*

Melissa

Made in the USA
Columbia, SC
13 June 2017